THE FOLK ROOTS
OF
CONTEMPORARY AFRO-AMERICAN POETRY
(Broadside Critics Series Number 3.
James A. Emanuel, General Editor)

ABOUT THE SERIES COVER

The cord represents literary creativity which has a strong tradition among African peoples. The tradition is found in the great store of oral history, in the contextual writing which forms designs seen on buildings, calabashes and other useful objects. It is implicit in many figurative designs and sculpture.

Several times in the history of the people, the cord has been severed abruptly—but continues again in a rich store of literary works represented here in the Broadside Critics Series.

—Cledie Taylor

THE FOLK ROOTS

OF

CONTEMPORARY

AFRO-AMERICAN POETRY

by

Bernard W. Bell

bp

BROADSIDE PRESS
12651 Old Mill Place   Detroit, Michigan 48238

TO STERLING A. BROWN,
THE DEAN OF AFRO-AMERICAN LETTERS

Acknowledgments

Grateful acknowledgment is extended to:

Random House, Inc., for permission to quote from the following copyrighted works: *Shadow and Act* and *Invisible Man,* by Ralph Ellison; and "Blueprint for Negro Literature," by Richard Wright, from *Amistad 2,* edited by John A. Williams and Charles F. Harris.

Dodd, Mead and Company, Inc., for permission to quote from *The Complete Poems of Paul Laurence Dunbar,* by Paul Laurence Dunbar.

Black World for permission to reprint "Contemporary Afro-American Poetry as Folk Art" from its March 1973 issue.

The University of Massachusetts, Amherst, for a faculty grant to help defray research expenses.

This study also owes a great debt to the inspiration and example of Professor Sterling A. Brown, whose wit and wisdom helped me clarify my thinking on the relationship of contemporary Afro-American poetry to folk art.

A very special, heartfelt thanks goes to my wife, Carrie, whose unerring eye and hand have helped to whittle down this manuscript into final shape.

Table of Contents

Introduction

Groping toward a realization of Afro-American genius, James Weldon Johnson—like W. E. B. DuBois, Alain Locke and other elder statesmen of the Harlem Renaissance —believed that a "demonstration of intellectual parity by the Negro through the production of literature and art"[1] would serve to eliminate racism. History has not vindicated this faith in "high art," Western reason, or American egalitarianism. Yet some of the most impressive poems by Robert Hayden, Gwendolyn Brooks, Melvin Tolson, Mari Evans, Audre Lorde, Etheridge Knight and other Black poets of the 1960's unquestionably fall within the tradition of high art. All art arises more or less in response to vital human needs. To denigrate the literary progenitors of the current Black Arts Movement or to dismiss their artifacts as mediocre tells us more about the politics and sensibilities of the critic than about the aesthetic qualities of specific works.[2] I do not pretend to be above the struggle to define the nature and function of Afro-American literature. I do not intend, however, to become embroiled here in the controversy of whether Black artists and critics of yesteryear were compelled by historical circumstances to go through the stage of affirming their personal and national identity by aspiring to the ideals of high art. Instead, my major purpose is to reveal why and how contemporary Afro-American poetry makes use of folk materials.

It is obviously time to review our thinking on the general differences between high art and folk art and to examine closely the relationship of Afro-American poetry published during 1962-1972 to the differences. Such an examination, to be useful, should emphasize several points: 1) the distinctions between European and American concepts of high art and folk art, 2) the principal theory of folk art that influenced 19th century Anglo-American writers in their quest for an indigenous art, 3) the ideas about folk art that characterized the attempts of DuBois, Locke, Johnson, Wright, Ellison and Baraka to define the relationship of Afro-American art to American culture, and 4) the techniques by which folk materials, especially music, were transformed into art by several well-known contemporary Afro-American poets.

In its broadest sense, high art connotes formal literature as well as music, dance and the graphic arts. But in this study, we will limit our attention to poetry. "Language," as René Wellek and Austin Warren remind us in *Theory of Literature,* "is the material of literature as stone or bronze is of sculpture, paints of pictures, or sounds of music. But one should realize that language is not mere inert matter like stone but is itself a creation of man and is thus charged with the cultural heritage of a linguistic group."[3] No scholar would argue that Afro-Americans and Anglo-Americans do not belong to the same Indo-European linguistic group. By the same token, no serious student of the Black experience would deny the obvious social and psychological differences in the cultural heritage of the two ethnic groups— deeply ingrained differences that have been manipulated by the WASP majority to perpetuate either an Olympian contempt or paternalistic tolerance of Black American character and culture. I shall return to this point later.

But now I shall focus on the Western concept of high art. Though the line between natural genius and madness is sometimes wafer thin and though poetry lovers may not always agree with the political or ethical content of all they hear, those who flock to readings of Ginsberg, McKuen, Yevtushenko, Baraka, and Gwendolyn Brooks are hardly inclined to dismiss these artists as mad or to endorse a policy of political censorship that would stifle the development of the arts. This in part explains the unpopularity of Plato's contempt for poets as expressed in the *Republic* and *Ion*. Critics have found a more viable concept of the art of poetry in Aristotle. It is in the *Poetics* that we find the definition of formal art, in particular tragedy, as "an imitation of an action that is serious, complete, and of a certain magnitude; in language embellished with each kind of artistic ornament, the several kinds being found in separate parts of the play; in the form of action, not of narrative; through pity and fear effecting the proper purgation of these emotions."[4] Basing his observations on the indigenous literature of Greece, Aristotle further expressed the conviction that the truth of poetry is more philosophical or universal than history, which concerns itself with the particular.

Horace, the conservative Roman critic who became the favorite of the Renaissance and Neo-classical periods, rigidly codified many of Aristotle's observations. The *Art of Poetry* reads like a rule book for critics and writers. Rather than imitate Nature, Horace advised the aspiring artist to study the Greek masterpieces, avoid extreme language, adhere to traditional themes, and cultivate moderation and decorum of style at all times. But the charm of poetry, he cautioned, does not necessarily exist for its own sake. The poet must blend the delightful and the useful, for teaching is also his business.[5]

Assuming that the nature and function of literature must be correlative, some modern aestheticians have taken issue with Horace. Much of the misunderstanding about the function of poetry, we are told in *Theory of Literature,* is buried in the Horatian caveat of *dulce et utile:* poetry delights and instructs. "When a work of literature functions successfully," Wellek and Warren argue, "the two 'notes' of pleasure and utility should not merely coexist but coalesce. The pleasure of literature . . . is not one preference among a long list of possible pleasures but is a 'higher pleasure' because pleasure in a higher kind of activity, i.e., non-acquisitive contemplation. And the utility—the seriousness,

13

the instructiveness—of literature is a pleasurable seriousness, i.e., not the seriousness of a duty which must be done
or of a lesson to be learned but an aesthetic seriousness, a
seriousness of perception."[6] In this reformulation of the
Horatian sugar-coated-pill theory of poetry, Wellek and
Warren provide the classic arena for the academic defense
of art-for-art's sake.

Turning from high art, the cult of beauty and taste, to
folk art, we immediately sense the dialectic tension between
the two concepts. But it is an oversimplification of the dy-
namics of this dialectic to reduce it to the mere question of
whether the work is the product of a conscious artist. Folk
art is the creative expression of the people, by the people,
for the people. Aristotle realized that Homer's *Odyssey* and
Iliad were originally folk epics performed by bards whose
purpose was to entertain and instruct their audience while
preserving their national heritage. In written form, this oral
literature loses its anonymity of authorship and takes on a
hybrid character. This transition is not easy to describe and
it most certainly defies dogmatic classifications.

High art and folk art are both concerned with the
truth of human experience, but the latter—as the early
poems of Wordsworth and Scott vividly illustrate—is a
more direct, popular evocation of commonplace reality.
And while the high seriousness of much of the poetry of
Arnold stresses a morbid individualism and enduring sophistication, folk art emphasizes communal modes of perceiving and expressing the vital forces of life. In contrast
to the self-conscious sophistication of high art, folk art at its
best is characterized by effortless grace in form and style.
Its primary appeal—as serious devotees of Yeats or Joyce
or Frost will undoubtedly admit—is to a particular ethnic
or regional group. Yet it is the artist's fidelity to the particular, the concrete reality, that enables him to achieve the
universal. The verities of high art are not more profound,
nor are the two kinds of art necessarily mutually exclusive.
In fact, as James Weldon Johnson's "O Black and Unknown
Bards" and Jean Toomer's "Song of the Son" suggest, high
art and folk art when viewed as the antipodes of a single

continuum, are inextricably bound to each other. Both of the above poems address themselves to the fundamental question of identity, celebrate the genius of the first New World Blacks, and capture in self-conscious yet felicitous language the soulful nature of the spirituals.

But when talking about the American identity, one must note, as stated earlier, that the WASP majority has manipulated philosophy and science in an attempt to justify its treatment of Afro-Americans. The Puritan legacy with its distorted notion of sex and the arts, the Jeffersonian-Rousseauistic view of natural rights with its ethnocentric egalitarianism, and the hydra-headed system of capitalism are commonly recognized as the cornerstones of the American ethos. Caught in this juggernaut of social forces, Africa and her progeny fell victim to the myth of an ignoble past and were cast by Europeans and Anglo-Americans alike as archetypal scapegoats on a Manichean world stage on which the victims represented evil. Allegorically, Black people were envisioned as the embodiment of absolute spiritual truths—e.g., Rousseau's Noble Savage or Melville's Babo—that graphically confirmed the white man's privileged relationship to his God and his alleged superiority to non-white men. The tensions between Puritan theology and the vested economic interests of the pioneers of the New World galvanized into the cultural matrix for the development of American character.

CHAPTER I

The Herderian Folk Ideology

In "The Roots of American Culture," Constance Rourke traces the folk philosophy of literature from Montaigne to Herder and concludes that Herder's theory of folk art went unnoticed in America until some of the Transcendentalists and Walt Whitman saw its major implications.[1] Picking up where Miss Rourke left off, Gene Bluestein's *The Voice of the Folk: Folklore and American Literary Theory* (1972) develops these observations into an intriguing thesis. According to Bluestein, the folk ideology of Johann Gottfried von Herder (1744-1803), critic, philosopher and folklorist, had a significant impact on the thinking of 19th century writers and scholars in their quest for a national literature. Both Emerson and Whitman, for example, found the then radical notion of folk art, especially folk song, as the base of a nation's formal literature compatible with their own ideas and efforts.[2] Unlike Rousseau, who also emphasized the value of "primitive" cultures but with the corollary notion that civilization destroys them, Herder, as Bluestein rightly points out, "does not suggest nostalgia for some irretrievable golden age; the importance of his point of view lies in his emphasis upon the persistence within contemporary society of folk traditions and his argument that a national literature can be attained only through building upon them."[3] As Chapters II and III will show, historically Afro-American aestheticians have been influenced by both the antiquarianism of Rousseau and the organicism of Herder, but during the current Black Arts Movement the Herderian view seems to prevail.

During the late eighteenth century when Germany was politically fragmented and culturally dominated by the French, Herder boldly argued that "unless our literature is founded on our *Volk,* we shall write eternally for closet sages and disgusting critics out of whose mouths and stomachs we shall get back what we have given."[4] Aware of Herder's strong objections to the intermixing of communities of diverse ethnic origins and his frequent use of biological terms like "organic" and "genetic," which he did not use in the sense of modern biology, one may wrongly infer that he was advocating racial purity. But, as F. M. Barnard explains in *Herder's Social and Political Thought,* Herder's "main concern was the historical continuity of a *Volk,* and he identified this continuity with the conscious transmission of social cultures and not with physical characteristics that attend heredity. He held this transmission to be 'genetic' because language via education made it possible to effect a linking of a *Volk's* social heritage between one generation and another, and 'organic' by virtue of the manner in which it was assimilated and creatively re-applied."[5] He thought language at once the expression of the individuality of each human being and the psychological matrix in which man's consciousness of his distinctive social heritage was aroused and deepened.[6] It must be remembered, therefore, "that it was not blood but language which Herder regarded as the essential criterion of a *Volk. Volk* was conceived as an ethnic not as a racial community."[7] A closer examination of the term *Volk* reveals that Herder generally

> drew a distinction between *Volk* and *Pobel* (rabble) on the one hand, and *Volk* and the intellectuals on the other. . . . In effect, then, Herder distinguishes between two *Volk* elements, the majority, consisting of the *bourgeoisie (das Volk der Burger),* and the minority, consisting of the intellectuals *(das Volk der Gelehrsamkeit).* The *Burger* are, however, not only the most numerous, but also . . . the most useful and venerable of the *Volk,* if not, indeed, the *Volk* proper. Herder associates with the term *Burger* all those occupations that figure prominently in folk-song: the farmer, the fisherman, the craftsman and artisan, the small trader; all those, that is, who, he feels, are least affected by the influence of 'civilization' and, accordingly, embody most truly the original *Volk* characteristics of the nation . . . such as spontaneity, [and] 'earthiness.' . . ."[8]

In a different time and place and under different circumstances, Dunbar, Johnson, McKay, Hughes and Brown were also to celebrate the virtues of folksong and the common man.

As exemplified in his *Humanität,* Herder later shifted his philosophical emphasis from diversity to universal unity. "The sort of international 'unity' that Herder had in mind," Barnard tells us, "was essentially the consciousness of common interests, needs, and purposes of diverse nations, each of which had a natural right to separate and independent existence. . . . What was at stake was the *growth* of unity out of and amidst diversity. . . . *Humanität,* in short, had to become an operative force in the life of every single individual, which, though unique in every particular case, carried within itself the seed of universal harmony."[9] In addition to the forces of ideas, Herder posited the concept of *Zeitgeist* as a source of transforming power. At times *Zeitgeist* is identified with the genius of *Humanität,* a "mighty genius," and a powerful demon. And at other times it is interpreted as the "sum of the thoughts, attitudes, strivings, drives, and living forces, expressing themselves with given causes and effects in a definite course of events."[10] These ideas regarding self-consciousness, diversity, interaction, and genius are, as we shall see, related in principle to those debated during the Harlem Renaissance of the Twenties and the Black Arts Movement of the Sixties.

Herder, unlike Rousseau, did not exalt the unsophistication of the folk mind, but expressed the view that "Nature has conferred another beneficent gift on our species, in leaving to such of its members as are least stored with ideas the first germs of superior sense, exhilarating music . . . and among the uncultivated nations, music is the first of the fine arts, by which every mind is moved. . . . But music, however rude and simple, speaks to every human heart, and this with the dance, constitutes Nature's general festival throughout the earth . . . they are instructive to the investigators of man; for the music of a nation, in its most imperfect form and favourite tunes, displays the internal character of the peoples."[11] In part this explains Herder's praise of the Biblical songs, which along with his other ideas about nationalism, poetry, language and folk music was available in translation to American artists and scholars early in the nineteenth century.[12] It is not surprising, then, that his influence is found in Emerson's *Journal* (1826), *Nature* (1836) and *The American Scholar* (1837) as well as in Whitman's *Leaves of Grass* (1855) and *A Backward Glance O'er Travel'd Roads* (1888). Passing on Herder's legacy, Whitman ends the latter work as follows: "Concluding with two items for the imaginative genius of the West, when it worthily rises—First, what Herder taught to the young Goethe, that really great poetry is always (like the Homeric or Biblical canticles) the result of a national spirit, and not the privilege of a polish'd and select few; Second, that the strongest and sweetest songs yet remain to be sung."[13]

CHAPTER II

Folk Art
and the
Harlem Renaissance

Major attempts by Afro-American academicians and
artists to identify the strengths of Afro-American folk art
and its potentialities for a Black American tradition of high
art have been strikingly similar to the spirit if not the letter
of Herder's folk ideology. I have found no documentary
evidence that W. E. B. DuBois, Alain Locke or James
Weldon Johnson—the elder statesmen of the Harlem Renaissance of the Twenties—nor Richard Wright, Ralph Ellison or Imamu Amiri Baraka (LeRoi Jones)—the spiritual
fathers of the Black Arts Movement of the Sixties—had
read Herder. But there is more than adequate circumstantial
evidence that they were familiar with Anglo-American in-

terpretations of Herder's theory that folk art laid the base for high art and the corollary concept of folksong as a spontaneous, indigenous expression of the collective soul of a people.

Interpretations of the pronouncements by Herder and the Grimm brothers generated a controversy in Europe over the concepts of group or folk poetry and individual or art poetry. Toward the close of the nineteenth century the group or communal theory was appropriated by scholars in America and applied to the ballads. Spearheaded by the scholarship and example of Francis James Child,[1] Francis Barton Gummere,[2] and George Lyman Kittredge,[3] Harvard University became the bastion of communalists. "The orthodox communalist," writes D. K. Wilgus in *Anglo-American Folksong Scholarship Since 1898*, "held that folk poetry is a genre which precedes and is antithetical to the poetry of art, that it springs spontaneously from a people, and that it is composed collectively by the people."[4] Of the three proponents, only Gummere seems to have been orthodox. Child, Wilgus reveals, "explicitly denied three fundamental tenets of the communalists: that ballads were dance songs, that they were of group authorship, and that they originated among the peasantry or in a classless society."[5] What Child actually believed was that " 'truly national or popular poetry' developed in a stage of society in which 'there is such a community of ideas and feelings that the whole people form one individual.' . . . This community of thought and feeling (not the homogeneous society of his followers) explains why the composition of one man 'will always be an expression of the mind and heart of a people as an individual and never the personality of individual men.' "[6] Both Gummere and Kittredge were disciples of Child. And while Gummere was the more prolific and ingenious scholar, Kittredge seems to have influenced more communalists,[7] including DuBois, Locke and Johnson.

Modern ballad scholarship is said to have begun with Kittredge. He kept the faith with the assumptions and conclusions of Child and Gummere, but impressed a generation of scholars who eventually disproved his statement that bal-

21

lad-making and ballad-singing were lost arts. It was Kittredge who gave academic validity to the antiquarian (Rousseauistic) revision of Herder's ideas when he wrote in the Introduction to the abridged *English and Scottish Popular Ballads* (1904):

> ... quite apart from what we call literature, there is a great mass of miscellaneous song and story which circulates among those who have neither books nor newspapers. To this oral literature ... education is no friend. Culture destroys it, sometimes with amazing rapidity. When a nation learns to read, it begins to disregard its traditional tales; it feels a little ashamed of them; and finally it loses both the will and the power to remember and transmit them. . . . To this oral literature belong the popular ballads, and we are justified, therefore, in calling them 'folk poetry.' They are not, like written literature, the exclusive possession of the cultivated classes in any community. They belonged, in the first instance, to the whole people, at a time when there were no formal divisions of literate and illiterate; when the intellectual interests of all were substantially identical, from the king to the peasant. As civilization advanced, they were banished from the polite society, but they lived on among the humble, among shepherds and ploughboys and 'the spinsters and knitters in the sun,' until even these became too sophisticated to care for them and they were heard no more.[8]

Kittredge also described the characteristic method of ballad composition "as improvisation in the presence of a sympathetic company which may even, at times, participate in the process," but went on to concede:

> It makes no difference whether a given ballad was in fact composed in the manner described, or whether it was composed (or even written) in solitude, provided the author belonged to the folk, derived his material from popular sources, made his ballad under the inherited influence of the method described, and gave it to the folk as soon as he had made it,—and provided, moreover, the folk accepted the gift and subjected it to that course of oral tradition which ... is essential to the production of a genuine ballad.[9]

Stirred by the vitality of Afro-American folksong, their own ivy league education, travels abroad and quest for a new phase of group development, DuBois, Locke and Johnson creatively applied the implications of Herder's theories (as refracted through the prism of Kittredge's pronouncements) to the spirituals, sermons, blues and jazz.

It is important to remember that most 19th century scholars and folklorists rejected the notion of Afro-American culture, paradoxically identifying Black American music as African and imitative Anglo-American music.[10] The fact that most early collections of slave songs were spirituals and rarely included ballads also confused white academicians and encouraged them to exclude Afro-American music from the American canon of folksong. Among the first to part the veil of ignorance and celebrate the virtues of the spirituals was DuBois.

William Edward Burghardt DuBois graduated from Fisk University in 1888 and went on to earn his Ph.D. from Harvard in 1895. He also spent two years (1892-94) of rigorous study at the University of Berlin. While in Germany, he visited Strasbourg, where Herder and Goethe had begun their lifelong friendship; Rheinpfalz, where he "had an excellent opportunity to study the peasant life closely and compare it with country life in the South";[11] and Weimar, where Herder had spent his final years in the court of Duke Karl August.[12] Before returning to the United States, DuBois also toured parts of Italy, Venice, Poland and France. Considering his ambitious pursuit of knowledge in several disciplines at a time when William James, Josiah Royce, George Santayana, Francis Child, Albert Bushnell Hart and George Lyman Kittredge were the great minds of Harvard, and considering his training and travels on the continent, it is unlikely that DuBois remained untouched by the spirit and thought of Herder, Goethe, and Rousseau.

The Souls of Black Folk, published in 1903, was a history-making collection of essays. It had, as James Weldon Johnson stated, "a greater effect upon and within the Negro race in America than any other single book published in this country since *Uncle Tom's Cabin.*"[13] More pertinent to our concern is the affirmation of a spiritual Black community revealed in the title, structure and biblical style of the book. Identifying himself in the Forethought as "bone of the bone and flesh of the flesh of them that live within the Veil," DuBois, in fourteen chapters each prefaced by a brief passage of poetry and a bar of the Sorrow Songs, outlines the spiritual world in which Black Americans struggle to survive. "They that walked in darkness," he writes in the chapter on folksongs, "sang songs in the olden days— Sorrow Songs—for they were weary at heart. And so before each thought that I have written in this book I have set a phrase, a haunting echo of these weird old songs in which the soul of the Black slave spoke to men."[14] Proclaiming Afro-American folksong "the singular spiritual heritage of the nation and the greatest gift of the Negro people," Du-Bois restates in Afro-American terms Herder's ideas on the importance of folk music as a window into the souls of a people and as the basis of a new nation's formal art. He considers the music essentially African in origin, recognizes its progressive hybridization and describes the creative process of the spirituals in much the same manner as Kittredge does ballad-making: "As in olden times, the words of these hymns were improvised by some leading minstrel of the religious band. The circumstances of the gathering, however, the rhythm of the songs, and the limitations of allowable thought, confined the poetry for the most part to single or double lines, and they seldom were expanded to quatrains or longer tales, although there are some few examples of sustained efforts, chiefly paraphrases of the Bible."[15] The essay "Of the Sorrow Songs" alludes to the existence of secular Afro-American music—including the debased "minstrel" and "coon" songs—but de-emphasizes their importance. In later years as editor of the *Crisis* (1910-1933) DuBois championed the cause of high art but encouraged Black Americans to turn to their usable past for inspiration and originality.

Like DuBois, Alain Leroy Locke was nurtured in high art but had a deep affinity for Afro-American folk art. He, too, was educated at Harvard (A.B. 1907, Ph.D. 1918) and the University of Berlin (1910-11). Trained in philosophy, Locke was the first Black Rhodes Scholar (1907-10).

During and subsequent to his three years at Oxford University, he became a frequent visitor to the capitals of the world and drank deeply at the fountains of Western culture. It is reasonable to assume, therefore, that Locke was familiar with the philosophical and folkloristic formulations of Herder and Kittredge. In 1916 Locke began a long, distinguished career as Professor of Philosophy at Howard University. And as editor of the Bronze Booklets and author of numerous articles and books[16] he was among the first to hail the Black American's spiritual Coming of Age.

The New Negro (1925), edited by Locke, is considered the landmark of the Harlem Renaissance. It not only celebrated what Locke optimistically described as "the attainment of a significant and satisfying new phase of group development" by Americans of African descent, but also revealed a vastly modified form of Herderian folk ideology and cultural pluralism. It disclosed an emphasis on the dignity of oppressed groups (the common man) and on the vitality of folk art; an effort to establish the legitimacy of racial expression, including the functional character of Afro-American folksongs, as a response to particular experience in American history; and finally, an attempt to relate the significance of Harlem, as a community of diverse elements and an emerging common consciousness, to its prototypes in the cultures of other nations.

To Locke, Negro youth spoke out of "a unique experience and with a particular representativeness." In the vanguard of a new cultural awakening, they embodied the potentiality of bridging the gap between folk and high art. "All classes of a people under social pressure are permeated with a common experience," Locke writes; "they are emotionally welded as others cannot be. With them, even ordinary living has epic depth and lyric intensity, and this, their material handicaps, is their spiritual advantage. So, in a day when art has run to classes, cliques, and coteries, and life lacks more and more a vital common background, the Negro artist, out of the depths of his group and personal experience, has to his hand almost the conditions of a classical art."[17] In other words, the Afro-American folk tradition is the distillation of the Black American's struggle to survive in an alien and hostile environment. This was the reality behind Locke's observation that the Negro of his day relied "upon the race-gift as a vast spiritual endowment from which our best developments have come and must come."[18] It is important to remember, however, that race as objectively employed by the younger generation was not, in Locke's view, a provincial cul-de-sac, but, "an idiom of experience, a sort of added enriching adventure and discipline, giving subtler overtones to life, making it more beautiful and interesting, even if more poignantly so. So experienced, it affords a deepening rather than a narrowing of social vision."[19] Digging "deep into the racy peasant undersoil of the race life" in order to free themselves from the distorted dialect of the minstrel tradition, the poets of the period "carried the folk-gift to the altitudes of art."[20] In short, what Locke sensed in the "flavor of language, flow of phrase, accent of rhythm in prose, verse and music, color and tone of imagery, idiom and timbre of emotion and symbolism" was the ambition and promise of Black artists to make a distinctive contribution to the general development of national art.[21]

The most acclaimed product of the race genius in America during the Harlem Renaissance was the spirituals. "But," as Locke points out, "the very elements which make them uniquely expressive of the Negro make them at the same time deeply representative of the soil that produced them. Thus, as unique spiritual products of American life, they become nationally as well as racially characteristic."[22] The creator of these folk songs, he believes, "worked them up from the 'shout' and the rhythmic elements of the sensuous dance." But out of this humble origin emanate an epic intensity and tragic profundity for which Locke says "the only historical analogy is the spiritual experience of the Jews and the only analogue, the Psalms."[23] On the other hand, he felt that the exquisite combination of Christian sentiment and music found in the spirituals ranks them with the Latin hymns, Gregorian tunes and the rarest of German chorals.[24] And though he expressed reservations about the spirituals as poetry, Locke maintained that their broken dialect and grammar were invariably the results of an instinctive euphonic sense in following the requirements of the musical rhythm.[25]

With full knowledge of the folk song origins of the European classics, Locke, DuBois, and Johnson were convinced that the Black musician who sustained the best traditions of the spirituals and organized their distinctive elements in a formal way would be the musical giant of his age. In the past the chief bond between Black Americans had been a common condition rather than a common consciousness. However, like Garvey and DuBois, Locke saw Afro-Americans as "the advance-guard of the African peoples" and Harlem as the cultural capital of the race. "In Harlem," he declares, "Negro life is seizing upon its first chances for group expression and self determination. It is —or promises at least to be—a race capital. That is why our comparison is taken with those nascent centers of folk-expression and self-determination which are playing a creative part in the world today. Without pretense to their political significance, Harlem has the same role to play for the New Negro as Dublin has had for the New Ireland or Prague for the New Czechoslovakia."[26] Thus Locke was among the first cultural historians to see Harlem as the key community in Black America and in his own unique way affirmed Herder's belief that the highest cultural values are to be found in the lowest orders of society.

Equally important for his personal example as well as his thoughts on folk art during the Harlem Renaissance was James Weldon Johnson. He was imbued with a deep sense of respect for high art by his West Indian cultural background, cosmopolitan tutors and New England teachers at Atlanta University, where he graduated in 1894.[27] At the same time, he was no stranger to the folk culture of Georgia, where he taught during his summer recess from college. And in his home town in Jacksonville, Florida, he was equally inspired by the urbane music of Ebenezer Methodist Episcopal Church, the chanted sermons of revivalist preachers and the African music of "ring-shouters."[28] Curiously enough, of all the books he read as a youth "the stories by the Brothers Grimm made the deepest effect."[29] In 1900, he wrote the lyrics to "Lift Every Voice and Sing," the Negro National Anthem. Then, under the influence of Dunbar and teamed with his brother Rosamond and a friend, Bob Cole, Johnson blossomed into one of the leading writers of musical comedy tunes in dialect. Also about this time, he discovered Whitman's *Leaves of Grass*. "I was engulfed and submerged by the book, and set floundering again,"[30] he wrote. It was the impact that Whitman had on him which triggered the realization of the artificiality of conventional Negro dialect poetry. After touring Paris and London, Johnson returned to New York to study dramatic literature and creative writing under Brander Matthews at Columbia University. The main fruit of these early years as a folk art enthusiast, popular song-writer for the theater, and poet was *The Autobiography of an Ex-Coloured Man*.

Published anonymously in 1912, *The Autobiography of an Ex-Coloured Man* is the story of Negro soul denied. The special genius of Johnson's protagonist—the product of an interracial union who ultimately decides to "pass" for white—is that he is equally adept at ragtime and Chopin. His unrealized dream was to write symphonic music based on ragtime and the old slave songs. Johnson's protagonist was potentially, in effect, the fictional embodiment of Herder's folk ideology.

While collecting folk material to transform into formal art, the nameless protagonist—a nominal prototype of Ellison's hero in *Invisible Man*—encounters two legendary folk types: John Brown, the old preacher, and "Singing Johnson," the creator of spirituals. Both are impressive men, ingenious and eloquent in their respective arts. In the Preface to *God's Trombones* (1927), seven sermons in verse, Johnson outlines the character and art of the folk preacher:

> The old-time Negro preacher of parts was above all an orator, and in good measure an actor. He knew the secret of

oratory, that at bottom it is a progression of rhythmic words more than it is anything else. Indeed, I have witnessed congregations moved to ecstasy by the rhythmic intoning of sheer incoherencies. He was a master of all the modes of eloquence. He often possessed a voice that was a marvelous instrument, a voice he could modulate from a sepulchral whisper to a crashing thunder clap. His discourse was generally kept at a high pitch of fervency, but occasionally he dropped into colloquialisms and, less often, into humor. He preached a personal and anthropomorphic God, a sure-enough heaven and a red-hot hell. His imagination was bold and unfettered. He had the power to sweep his hearers before him; and so himself was often swept away. At such times his language was not prose but poetry.[31]

The folk preacher did not preach a formal sermon from a formal text; the text more often than not served as a starting point and frequently had no relation to the development of the sermon, which was delivered in an electrifying, rhythmic manner. Johnson's innovative use of these folk sermons will be discussed in Chapter IV.

A full description of "Singing Johnson" and the tradition of the Black bards of old dominates the Preface to *The Book of American Negro Spirituals* (1925):

"Singing" Johnson is one of the indelible pictures on my mind. A small but stocky, dark-brown man was he, with one eye, and possessing a clear, strong high-pitched voice. . . . A maker of songs and a wonderful leader of singing. A man who could improvise lines on the moment. . . . "Singing" Johnson was of the line of the mightier bards of an earlier day, and he exemplified how they worked and how the Spirituals were "composed." These bards, I believe, made the original inventions of story and song, which in turn were influenced or modified by the group in action.[32]

This tradition, as we may recall, has a strong affinity to that advanced by Kittredge for ballad-making.[33]

It is also important that in the Preface to *The Book of American Negro Poetry* (first published in 1922) Johnson advocates one of the most challenging approaches to folk art of his day. In an apparent attempt to reconcile the differences between folk art and high art, he argues that Afro-American folksongs represent a vast mine of material to be tapped by some genius of the race. Unlike many of his urbane contemporaries, Johnson affirmed the cultural values of the blues and jazz. By folksongs, he meant sacred and secular music, the spirituals and ragtime. (He seems to have used the term "ragtime" to designate a potpourri of musical types, including work songs, blues, and jazz.) [34] And the genius he extols is both national and international in character. The music created through the transmuting power—Herder's Zeitgeist?—of Black artists would be not only the soul of their race, but the soul of America. "This power of the Negro to suck up the national spirit from the soil," Johnson writes, "and create something artistic and original, which, at the same time, possesses the note of universal appeal, is due to a remarkable racial gift of adaptability; it is more than adaptability, *it is a transfusive quality. And the Negro has exercised this transfusive quality not only here in America, where the race lives in larger numbers, but in European countries, where the number has been almost infinitesimal.*" [35] The apparent contradiction here is resolved if we acknowledge the creative potentialities of the common man and the reality of the socially induced ethnic and nationalistic tensions mirrored in Afro-American poetry. The parallels between these ideas and Herder's cultural democracy and nationalism seem to me stronger than mere coincidence allows.

Johnson's comments on the significance of an indigenous language are also related to Herder's views. Observing that the newer Negro poets were trying to break away not from Negro dialect but from the limitations imposed on it by the plantation and minstrel traditions, Johnson writes:

> What the colored poet in the United States needs to do is something like what Synge did for the Irish; he needs to find a form that will express the racial spirit by symbols from within rather than without, such as the mere mutilation of English spelling and pronunciation. He needs a form that is freer and larger than dialect, but which will still hold the racial flavor; a form expressing the imagery, the idioms, the peculiar turns of thought, and the distinctive humor and pathos, too, of the Negro, but which will also be capable of voicing the deepest and highest

emotions and aspirations, and allowing of the widest range of subjects and the widest scope of treatment.[36]

These ideas are by no means an indiscriminate, direct adoption of Herder's linguistic nationalism, but they do highlight the spiritual bond reflected in a distinctive linguistic form and urge its development.

So far I have stressed the influence of European ideology. To avoid an oversimplistic discussion of the complex process of cross-cultural fertilization that has historically existed in one form or another among peoples of different cultures, let me at least cite the names of a few African and Caribbean precursors of negritude. As early as 1880 Edward Blyden, the Liberian nationalist, advocated the radical view that "Africa may yet prove to be the spiritual conservatory of the world."[37] He proudly proclaimed his preference for being an African "rather than a Greek in the time of Alexander, a Roman in the Augustan period, or an Anglo-Saxon in the nineteenth century." A classical scholar, Blyden firmly believed that "each race had its own peculiar assets, excelling in certain pursuits and less successful in others. Races were therefore not competitive or comparative so much as complementary, and in their totality they made up God's divinity."[38] Other pioneer cultural nationalists include J. E. Casely Hayford, J. E. K. Aggrey, Marcus Garvey, Nicolás Guillén, and Jean Price-Mars.[39]

I have attempted to isolate what was common in the thoughts of the elder statesmen of the Harlem Renaissance in order to highlight their points of contact with, and divergence from, Herderian folk ideology. But the last thing I wish to suggest is that Herder was the sole source of their ideas. As stated earlier, I have found no documentary evidence that DuBois, Locke, or Johnson included the works of Herder in their personal libraries. Nevertheless, their training, travels and writings provide more than adequate circumstantial evidence that in being in tune with the folk spirit of their age they were consciously or unconsciously in tune with the spirit of Herder's ideas on the relationship between folk art and formal art.

CHAPTER III

Folk Art
and the
Black Arts Movement

According to a poll of thirty-eight Black writers taken by *Negro Digest* in 1968, the most important Black American writer of all time is Richard Wright.[1] Ralph Ellison and Amiri Baraka also ranked high in the poll, with the latter selected as the most important living Black poet and playwright. No three Black writers are more different in their political persuasions and life styles than Wright, Ellison and Baraka. But each has embraced a folk ideology whose emphasis on ethnic consciousness, cultural pluralism, the vernacular, and music is of the home grown variety while at the same time, it seems to me, essentially Herderian.

During the Depression, Wright, a Southerner by birth

and upbringing, attempted the herculean feat of bridging the gap between Marxist and Black Nationalist ideologies. He encouraged Black writers to commit themselves to a revolutionary perspective of society and to turn to their folk heritage for inspiration. Recognizing the nationalistic implications of Afro-American life, he urged young Black writers to accept them in order to transcend rather than encourage them. In the past, Wright argued in "Blueprint for Negro Literature," Afro-American writing was, on the whole, "the voice of the educated Negro pleading with white America" that he was not an inferior human being.[2] Rarely had the best of this writing been addressed to the needs, sufferings and aspirations of the Afro-American (i.e., the common man) himself. But, Wright firmly believed, there was and is a culture of the Afro-American, rooted in the church and expressed in the oral literature of the people, which has always been addressed to him alone:

> It was . . . in a folklore moulded out of rigorous and inhuman conditions of life that the Negro achieved his most indigenous expression. Blues, spirituals, and folk tales recounted from mouth to mouth, the whispered words of a black mother to her black daughter on the ways of men, the confidential wisdom of a black father to his black son, the swapping of sex experiences on street corners from boy to boy in the deepest vernacular, work songs sung under blazing suns, all these formed the channels through which the racial wisdom flowed.[3]

Why, Wright asked, have Afro-American writers of the last century failed to continue and to deepen this folk vein? Why have they not "tried to create a more intimate and yet more social system of artistic communication between them and their people?"[4] His answer, of course, was political and psychological. Because Afro-American writers thought they could escape the fate of the Black masses through individual achievement, most of them shied away from ethnic consciousness. Thus, Wright concludes: "Two separate cultures sprang up: one for the Negro masses, crude, instinctive, unwritten, and unrecognized; and the other for the sons and daughters of a rising Negro bourgeoisie, bloodless, petulant, mannered, and neurotic."[5]

In truth, Wright straddled both of these cultures. "Middle-class Negroes," he writes in *White Man, Listen!*, "borrowed the forms of the culture which they strove to make their own, but the migratory Negro worker improvised his cultural forms and filled those forms with a content wrung from a bleak and barren environment, an environment that stung, crushed, all but killed him."[6] One might well take issue, as Ellison does, with Wright's portrayal of Afro-American life as unremittingly bleak and sterile. In fact Wright himself might be included in that small band of Negroes he sardonically yet accurately describes as rising through luck, diligence and courage to make "the culture of their nation their own even though that nation still rejected them."[7] And though he says he personally identified with the folksongs of the migrant Afro-American, his short stories, poems and novels bear the imprint of Anglo-American, European and even Japanese literary influences. What then are we to make of Wright's folk ideology? Perhaps the most revealing statement on the complexity of Wright's thoughts on folk art and high art appears in his "Blueprint for Negro Literature":

> In order to do justice to their subject matter, in order to depict Negro life in all of its manifold and intricate relationships, a deep, informed and complex consciousness is necessary, a consciousness which draws for its strength upon the fluid lore [oral tradition] of a great people, and moulds this lore with the concepts that move and direct the forces of history today. Every short story, novel, poem, and play should carry within its lines, implied or explicit, a sense of the oppression of the Negro people, the danger of war, of fascism, of the threatened destruction of culture and civilization; and, too, the faith and necessity to build a new world.[8]

Aware that no theory of life, including Marxism, can take the place of life itself or substitute for technique, Wright cautions Black writers:

> He may with disgust and revulsion, say no and depict the horrors of capitalism encroaching upon the human being. Or he may, with hope and passion, say yes and depict the faint stirrings of a new and emerging life. But in whatever social voice he chooses

34

to speak, whether positive or negative, there should always be heard or overheard his faith, his necessity. And this faith and necessity should not be simple or rendered in primer-like terms; for the life of the Negro people is not simple as some dyspeptic intellectuals contend. The presentation of their lives should be simple, yes; but all the complexity, the strangeness, the magic wonder of life that plays like a bright sheen over even the most sordid existence, should be there. To borrow a phrase from the Russians, it should have a *complex simplicity*. Eliot, Stein, Joyce, Hemingway and Anderson; Gorky, Barbusse, Nexo, and Jack London no less than the folklore of the Negro himself form the heritage of Negro writers. Every iota of gain in human sensibility and thought should be ready grist for the mill, no matter how far-fetched they may seem in their immediate implications. It would be a sad brigade of Negro writers who would be afraid of this; and it would be a limited consciousness that could not assimilate these influences.[9]

More than anything else this passage reveals Wright's attempt to synthesize these social and aesthetic beliefs. It also reveals the aesthetic sensibility that influenced Ellison—his repudiation of Wright notwithstanding—and Baraka in the Forties and Fifties; just as Hughes, Marxism, and the Chicago University sociologists[10] influenced Wright in the Thirties; as McKay and Johnson influenced Hughes in the Twenties; and as Dunbar and Whitman influenced Johnson at the turn of the century.[11]

Born in Oklahoma, named after Ralph Waldo Emerson, and trained as a symphony composer at Tuskegee Institute, Ralph Ellison has managed to successfully reconcile his folk and classical heritages. Before his fateful Harlem meeting with Wright in 1936, Ellison had already been immersed in the rich oral literature of the churches, schoolyards, barbershops, drug stores, and cotton-picking camps of his community. During his boyhood, Oklahoma City, one of the great centers for Southwestern jazz, was alive with the blues of Ma Rainey, Ida Cox and Clara Smith as well as the jazz of bands like that of King Oliver. But in school, young trumpet-playing Ellison was steeped in military and classical music. "It was most confusing," he admits; "the folk tradition demanded that I play what I heard and felt around me, while those who were seeking to teach the classical tradition in the schools insisted that I play strictly according to the book and express that which I was supposed to feel."[12] At Tuskegee Ellison was intrigued by *The Waste Land,* whose rhythms reminded him of jazz and whose classical allusions influenced his passion for literature.[13] It was Wright, however, who discussed the art of fiction with the young beginner and guided him to the prefaces of James and Conrad and to the letters of Dostoyevsky. It was Wright who introduced him to Malraux, Leadbelly and Marxism all in the same evening. And it was Wright who midwifed Ellison's first publication.

Shadow and Act, a collection of essays that appeared more than a decade after the monumental achievement of *Invisible Man,* contains Ellison's fullest formulation of a folk ideology for Afro-American writers. The essays are concerned with three general themes: literature and folklore, Afro-American music, and the complex relationship between the Afro-American sub-culture and American culture in general. Ellison feels that those writers who plead the Afro-American's humanity are indulging in a false issue. The real issue he perceives as the forms of our humanity and the elements of our background worth preserving. In "The Art of Fiction: An Interview" he tells us:

> The clue to this can be found in folklore, which offers the first drawings of any group's character. It preserves mainly those situations which have repeated themselves again and again in the history of any given group. It describes those rites, manners, customs and so forth, which insure the good life, or destroy it; and it describes those boundaries of feeling, thought and action which that particular group has found to be the limitation of the human condition. It projects this wisdom in symbols which express the group's will to survive; it embodies those values by which the group lives and dies. These drawings may be crude but they are nonetheless profound in that they represent the group's attempt to humanize the world. It's no accident that great literature, the products of individual artists, is erected upon this humble base.[14]

Whether by way of Emerson or DuBois or Eliot or Miss Rourke, this concept of the relationship between folk art and high art is distinctly Herderian.

But in contrast to Herder's stress on homogeneity as the key to cultural and national vitality, Ellison again and again points out the heterogeneous character of Afro-American culture and the complex relationship existing between it and the larger culture. And his argument is most persuasive:

> Negro folklore, evolving within a larger culture which regarded it as inferior, was an especially courageous expression. It announced the Negro's willingness to trust his own experience, his own sensibilities as to the definition of reality, rather than allow his masters to define these crucial matters for him. His experience is that of America and the West, and is as rich a body of experience as one would find anywhere. We can view it narrowly as something exotic, folksy or "low-down," or we may identify ourselves with it and recognize it as an important segment of the larger experience—not lying at the bottom of it, but intertwined, diffused in its very texture.[15]

One ironic example of the complexity and universality of Afro-American folk art, Ellison observes, is the singing of spirituals by the descendants of the men who enslaved us, as an exaltation of *their* humanity.[16]

Like DuBois, Locke, Johnson and Wright, Ellison is convinced "that the most authoritative rendering of America in music is that of American Negroes."[17] This music has been a unique blend of European styles and of cultural tendencies inherited from Africa. And for writers who drew on the slave songs, blues and jazz, the possibilities for formal literature were infinite. In some cases, he feels, Afro-American folksong captured the essence of "human situations so well that a whole corps of writers could not exhause their universality."[18] In the light of these convictions, it might be worth examining Ellison's comments on the art of Afro-American folksong.

More than any other modern student of folklore Ellison insists on the artistic qualities of Afro-American music. While DuBois, Locke and Johnson extolled Afro-American genius or soul, Ellison is more restrained. He is wistful about some genius doing as much with the slave songs as

Thomas Mann did with the Joseph story.[19] But as his use of genius implies, he generally stresses technique. And though the technique of the gospels (i.e., modernized spirituals), blues and jazz is not taught formally, Ellison strongly suggests that they are mastered only through immersion and apprenticeship in the complex tradition of Afro-American song. Using Mahalia Jackson as a paradigm, he takes great care in describing the complexity of the gospels:

> It is an art which depends upon the employment of the full expressive resources of the human voice—from the rough growls employed by blues singers, the intermediate sounds, half-cry, half-recitative, which are common to Eastern music; the shouts and hollers of American Negro folk cries; the rough-edged tones and broad vibratos, the high, shrill and grating tones which rasp one's ears like the agonized flourishes of flamenco, to the gut tones, which remind us of where the jazz trombone found its human source. It is an art which employs a broad rhythmic freedom and accents the lyric line to reinforce the emotional impact. It utilizes half-tones, glissandi, blue notes, humming and moaning. . . . Its diction ranges from the most precise to the near liquidation of word-meaning in the sound; a pronunciation which is almost of the academy one instant and of the broadest cotton-field dialect the next. And it is most eclectic in its use of other musical idiom; indeed, it borrows any effect which will aid in the arousing and control of emotion.[20]

The art of the gospel attests to the strength and vitality of Afro-American folksong and reveals itself as an eclectic art that recognizes no arbitrary boundary between secular and sacred modes of expression.

Ellison is equally serious and expansive in expressing his views on the blues and jazz. "The blues is an art of ambiguity," he argues, "an assertion of the irrepressibly human over all circumstance whether created by others or by one's own human failings. They are the only consistent art in the United States which constantly remind us of our limitations while encouraging us to see how far we can actually go. When understood in their more profound implication, they are a corrective, an attempt to draw a line upon man's own limitless assertion."[21] Praising the lyricism of the late Jimmy Rushing, Ellison demonstrates his point by reminding us that "when we listen to his handling of lyrics we become aware of that quality which makes for the mysteriousness of the blues: their ability to imply far more than they state outright and their capacity to make the details of sex convey meanings which touch upon the metaphysical. For, indeed, they always find poetry in the limits of the Negro vocabulary. . . . Jimmy," Ellison continues, "has always shown a concern for the correctness of language, and out of the tension between the traditional folk pronunciation and his training in school, he has worked out a flexibility of enunciation and a rhythmical agility with words which make us constantly aware of the meanings which shimmer just beyond the limits of the lyrics."[22] The communal aspect of this secular art form was most striking when blues singer, jazz band and dancers became one: "It was when Jimmy's voice began to soar with the spirit of the blues that the dancers—and the musicians—achieved that feeling of communion which was the true meaning of the public jazz dance. The blues, the singer, the band and the dancers formed the vital whole of jazz as an institutional form, and even today neither part is quite complete without the rest."[23]

Technique, then, was for Ellison the key to the creative vitality of Afro-American folksong. And whether gospel, jazz or blues, the source of the technique was a tension between the compulsion to express one's ethnic experience and the desire to master classical techniques. "In early jazz," for example, "these sounds found their fullest expression in the timbre of the blues voice, and the use of mutes, water glasses and derbies on the bells of their horns arose out of an attempt to imitate this sound."[24] The art of jazz thrives on improvisation. It is "an art of individual assertion within and against the group. Each true jazz moment . . . springs from a contest in which each artist challenges all the rest; each solo flight, or improvisation, represents . . . a definition of his identity: as individual, as member of the collectivity and as a link in the chain of tradition."[25] Seen in this light, folk art is a ritualistic process in which the individual is reconciled with the group.

In a very real sense, Ellison's own formal education in classical music and his personal experience with jazz were a prototype of this synthesis. He explains how he translated his dual heritage into literary expression in the now famous exchange with Stanley Edgar Hyman. He protests that he did not use folklore in *Invisible Man* because he was a Negro but because Eliot and Joyce made him aware of the literary value of his folk heritage. "My point," he says rather primly, "is that the Negro American writer is also an heir of the human experience which is literature, and this might well be more important to him than his living folk tradition. For me, at least, in the discontinuous, swiftly changing and diverse American culture, the stability of the Negro American folk tradition becomes precious as a result of an act of literary discovery. Taken as a whole, its spirituals along with its blues, jazz and folk tales, it has . . . much to tell us of the faith, humor and adaptability to reality necessary to live in a world which has taken on much of the insecurity and blues-like absurdity known to those who brought it into being. For those who are able to translate its meanings into wider, more precise vocabularies it has much to offer indeed."[26]

Understandably, Ellison contradicts himself in this collection of essays written over a period of almost twenty years. In 1953 when he was presented the National Book Award, he explained his rejection of the hard-boiled style of Hemingway:

> For despite the notion that its rhythms were those of everyday speech, I found that when compared with the rich babel of idiomatic expression around me, a language full of imagery and gesture and rhetorical canniness, it was embarrassingly austere. Our [i.e., Afro-American] speech I found resounding with an alive language swirling with over three hundred years of American living, a mixture of the folk, the Biblical, the scientific and the political. Slangy in one stance, academic in another, loaded poetically with imagery at one moment, mathematically bare of imagery in the next.[27]

In truth, then, Ellison was linked to his socio-cultural heritage by both the spoken and written word. More important, by word and deed he demonstrates that his chief mode for creatively transmitting the duality of his ethnic and national identity has been Afro-American speech.

The basic difference between Ellison's theory of Afro-American folksong and Amiri Baraka's formulation might be summed up in the questions "how" and "why." Ellison stresses the "how," the technique and form of the music, while Baraka probes into the "why," the socio-cultural philosophy that produced it. "The blues and jazz aesthetic, to be fully understood, must be seen in as nearly its complete context as possible," Baraka argues in *Black Music*. "People made bebop. The question the critic must ask is: why?"[28] The way the music is made is secondary. For without understanding the attitudes and emotional philosophy contained in Black music, one can not legitimately deal with its meaning and worth. For Baraka, as for Herder, the music of a nation is essentially the expression of a collection of attitudes about the world or the internal character of the people.

Amiri Baraka was educated at Howard University and Columbia University, where he studied comparative literature.[29] "For me," he wrote in 1959, "Lorca, Williams, Pound and Charles Olson have had the greatest influence. Eliot, earlier (rhetoric can be so lovely, for a time . . . but only remains so for the rhetorician). . . . We can get nothing from England. And the diluted formalism of the academy (the formal culture of the U.S.) is anaemic & fraught with incompetence & unreality."[30] Thus the early Baraka, an habitué of Greenwich Village, was also an heir of the human experience which is literature. And for him, as for Ellison, the tensions between folk and formal traditions were a pressing issue. Listen, for example, to the opening paragraph of the essay quoted above:

"How You Sound? ?" is what we recent fellows are up to. How *we* sound; our peculiar grasp on, say: a. Melican speech, b. Poetries of the world, c. Our selves (which is attitudes, logics, theories, jumbles of our lives, & all that), d. And the final . . . The Totality of Mind: Spiritual . . . God ? ? (or you name it): Social (zeitgeist): or Heideggerian *umwelt*.[31]

In the conflagration of the Sixties the Prodigal Son of Newark was baptized in Blackness and reborn Imamu Amiri Baraka, dubbed by some as the High Priest of the Black Arts Movement. Even so, Baraka was not able to divest himself completely of the influence of, in his words, "having read all of whitie's books."[32] The form of his thought is still Western even though the content might be Black. And when he discusses modern Black music, Herder's influence is evident. For example, in "The Changing Same (R & B and New Black Music)" he writes:

> Rhythm and Blues is part of the "national genius," of the Black man, of the Black nation. It is the direct, no monkey business expression of urban and rural (in its various stylistic variations) Black America.
> The hard, driving shouting of James Brown identifies a place and image in America. A people and an energy, harnessed and not harnessed by America. JB is straight out, open, and speaking from the most deeply religious people on this continent.[33]

Although the phrase "national genius" might well be derived from immediate American sources like Edward Sapir,[34] its seminal force emanates from Herder's metaphysical notion of *Zeitgeist*.

Assuming that the national genius of a people is inherent in their folksongs, the question remains: How is the genius or energy of the urbanized blues and spirituals translated into formal literature? The closest Baraka comes to answering this question is in "The Myth of a Negro Literature." If the Black American writer wants to tap his legitimate cultural tradition he should utilize "the entire spectrum of the American experience from the point of view of the emotional history of the black man in this country: as its victim and its chronicler."[35] He should explore "the soul of such a man, as it exists outside the boundaries of commercial diversion or artificial social pretense."[36] Baraka disdained "middle-brow" models and advised employing "recognizable tradition" only in certain contemporary usages. For example, among other things, rather than turning to English models Black poets would do better by listening to Bessie Smith or Billie Holiday. "For an American, black or white, to say that some hideous imitation of Alexander Pope means more to him, emotionally, than the blues of Ray Charles or Lightnin' Hopkins," Baraka states heatedly, "it would be required for him to have completely disappeared into the American Academy's vision of a Europeanized and colonial American culture, or to be lying."[37]

Baraka's thoughts on nationalism, of course, have a closer kinship with the teachings of DuBois, Garvey, Malcolm X and Fanon than they do with Herder's. For Herder, language was the chief criterion by which a group's identity as a separate social unit could be established. In contrast Baraka stresses three factors: color (race), culture and consciousness. "If we *feel* differently, we have different *ideas*," he maintains. "Race is feeling. Where the body, and the organs come in. Culture is the preservation of these feelings in superrational to rational form. Art is one method of expressing these feelings and identifying the form, as an emotional phenomenon."[38] On the surface this concept of an ethnic community is not only illogical but drastically different from Herder's linguistic nationalism. But when we recall that "Herder considered language to be at once the expression of the individuality of each human being and the psychological matrix in which man's consciousness of his distinctive social heritage was aroused and deepened,"[39] we realize that in its stress on inward forces of socio-political cohesion Herder's theory actually provided the ideological foundation for subsequent cultural nationalistic movements. Besides, Baraka's logic appears less preposterous if we accept the proposition that Black Americans do affirm certain feelings of identity and certain attitudes toward our situation as Americans. In this sense, Black proponents of Afro-American folk art agree, a collective group consciousness or spiritual bond is a reality. To link this social-psychological phenomenon to biological differences, however, is to court controversy.

This is not to suggest that the notion of the Negro as only an American, and nothing else, with "no values and culture to guard and protect,"[40] is historically sound. A more viable concept of the Black experience as an ethnic sub-culture is persuasively advanced in Milton Gordon's *Assimilation in American Life.* Ethnicity, according to Gordon, involves

> the social-psychological element of a special sense of both ancestral and future-oriented identification with the group. These are the "people" of my ancestors, therefore they are my people, and they will be the people of my children and their children. With members of other groups I may share political participation, occupational relationships, common civic enterprises, perhaps even an occasional warm friendship. But in a very special way, which history has decreed, I share a sense of indissoluble and intimate identity with *this group* and *not that one* within the society and the world.[41]

Since this concept of an ethnic community as a body of people with a "shared feeling of peoplehood" corresponds with the reality of the Black experience as we know it today, it is clearly more tenable than either the anachronistic view of Glazer and Moynihan or the logic of Amiri Baraka.

I have attempted an examination of the ideas of DuBois, Locke, Johnson, Wright, Ellison, and Baraka on Afro-American folk art. These ideas taken as a whole do not constitute a systematic theory of folk art. They are, nevertheless, of interest mainly for three reasons. They provide the necessary historical perspective to judge fairly the major attempts by Black Americans to reconcile Afro-American folk art with high art; secondly, they reveal the importance of Herder's theory of the relationship between folk art and formal literature to the quest for a distinctive national literature; and, thirdly, they establish Afro-American music as a valid criterion for evaluating the distinctive quality of Afro-American literature.

CHAPTER IV

Contemporary
Afro-American Poetry
as Folk Art

Contemporary Black American poets write out of a
tradition which Whitman, Dunbar, Johnson, Pound, Joyce,
Eliot, Hughes, Brown and E. E. Cummings, among others,
have helped to shape. Depending on socio-political circumstances and individual artistic sensibilities, they express
their bittersweet vision of the Black experience by either
adopting traditional forms or improvising new ones. In a
very real sense, however, contemporary Afro-American
poetry has its roots in the African slaves' lyrical affirmation
of life. For it is to the Afro-American spirituals and folksongs—a unique fusion of a centuries-old African sensibility
and an inchoate Puritan American culture—that America

45

is indebted for its most priceless music, those sorrowful and joyous songs that subtly yet forcefully decried oppression and celebrated the possibilities of the human spirit. And whatever is distinctively ethnic in the poetry of this generation of Black poets, I intend to demonstrate in this chapter, is attributable to the creative forces of this heritage. I further propose to show how the music of Black folk gets into a considerable amount of their poetry, especially poetry of the Sixties.

The consensus among many Black writers and critics affirms this influence of American folk art upon ethnic literature. This concept, as I have attempted to demonstrate, is largely derived from the nationalistic folk ideology of Herder. Given the democratic core of Herder's theory, it is surprising, as Constance Rourke points out in "The Roots of American Culture," that it did not create a ripple in American thinking until some Transcendentalists and, later, Walt Whitman recognized its importance! At the close of the 19th century, however, folk art theories became grist for the Harvard mill of ballad scholars like Francis James Child and George Lyman Kittredge, who supported the antiquarian revision of Herder's ideas in their respective editions of *The English and Scottish Popular Ballads*.[2]

For the past fifty years or more Black writers and critics have been moving toward the realization of a Black aesthetic. The path of this movement has never been smooth, nor have all the travelers been militant separatists. In fact, during the Harlem Renaissance of the Twenties the phrases "Black art" and "Black aesthetic" were non-existent; and most Black writers disavowed racial labels, which they felt constricted their humanity and artistic impulse. Nevertheless, as books like *The New Negro* disclose, DuBois, Locke, Johnson, Hughes, Cullen, Toomer, Brown and others were turning to Africa and Afro-American folk art as well as Europe for a sense of tradition. More to the point of this study, DuBois, Locke and Johnson were convinced that the Black artist who employed the distinctive elements of the spirituals in a formal way would be the artistic giant of his age.

46

In the Thirties Richard Wright attempted to connect Marxist and Black Nationalist ideologies. His "Blueprint for Negro Writing" urges Black writers to become revolutionary, to draw on their oral folk tradition to "create the myths and symbols that inspire a faith in life," and to place "cultural health above narrow sectional prejudices." In the late Forties, Léopold Sédar Senghor, moved by the spirit and example of the Harlem Renaissance poets,[3] gave a new vitality and international dimension to the concept of negritude, i.e., the French West African interpretation of the yet unarticulated Black aesthetic, with the publication of *Anthology of New Black and Madagascan Poetry*. While in Europe during the Fifties, Wright delivered a lecture entitled "The Literature of the Negro in the United States," in which he expanded on his earlier views of the two main streams of Afro-American expression. The politics of Wright's "Blueprint for Negro Writing" and standard lectures on Afro-American letters were anathema to many of his contemporaries, but his faith in folk art struck a more responsive chord.

Ralph Ellison, for example, is much less a social determinist. He feels Wright was overcommitted to ideology and defined the Black experience too narrowly in sociological terms. Ellison nevertheless wants many of the same things for his people that Wright wanted and feels it important to affirm those achievements which were of value beyond any question of segregation, economics or previous condition of servitude. Music heads the list, for to Ellison's mind the slave songs, blues and jazz have been the most authoritative evocation of America in music. He expresses the conviction in *Shadow and Act* that writers draw on "this humble base."

Wright's essay had a much more dramatic influence on the revolutionary commitment of Black Nationalist writers of the Sixties. This is most clearly evidenced in the cultural nationalism of Imamu Amiri Baraka. In "The Myth of a Negro Literature," Baraka updates and refocuses Wright's blueprint for Black writers. Intemperately attacking the whole corpus of Afro-American literature, Baraka asks: "Where is the Negro-ness of a literature written in imitation of the meanest of social intelligences to be found in American culture, i.e., the white middle class?"[4] Rather than make a commitment to "cultural relevance and intellectual purity," he notes, the Black writer has been essentially middle-brow and commercial. His writing is neither rooted in the reality of the Black experience nor addressed to the needs of Black people. Only the blues, jazz, and spirituals, Baraka feels, have been able "to survive the constant and willful dilutions of the black middle class."

On this point and a few others, Baraka gets carried away by the passion of his convictions. Although jazz does indeed draw "its strengths and beauties out of the depth of the black man's soul," its complex musical tradition—country blues, urban blues, down-home jazz, swing, bop, cool jazz, hard-bop, funky jazz, etc.—is hardly restricted to "the lowest classes of Negroes." I would also submit that professional writing is essentially a middle-class endeavor. And all artists must achieve some reasonable compromise between their artistic integrity and the demands of the marketplace. But the reader should not be turned off by Baraka's flair for iconoclasm, for buried beneath his sweeping indictment of Black American writers is the key to his literary manifesto: assuming that Black music is a synthesis of the Black American's African heritage and his American experience and that it addresses itself to the needs, sufferings and hopes of the Black masses, Baraka is suggesting that the best, if not the only, means of judging the quality of Blackness in literature is to compare it to the richness and vitality of Black music. "If there is ever a Negro literature," he concludes, "it must disengage itself from the weak, heinous elements of the culture that spawned it, and use its very existence as evidence of a more profound America."[5] This was the revolutionary challenge for Black writers in the Sixties.

Let us return for a moment to Baraka's indictment of Afro-American literature. Whatever the shortcomings of our early literary efforts, they ought not be considered in the main as the reprehensible fumblings of middle-class social-climbers. For, like Black American music, they sprang from a unique fusion of African and American legacies and constitute part of a fresh cultural configuration. Take Paul Laurence Dunbar. He frequently wrote in the local color tradition of James Whitcomb Riley, Irwin Russell and Thomas Nelson Page, but poems like "An Ante-Bellum Sermon," "Black Samson of Brandywine," and "Philosophy" give evidence of a depth of sensitivity and point of view not apparent in his white models. And as his craftsmanship developed, his poetry moved farther from the more superficial aspects of the dialect tradition, even though his achievements in standard English and traditional forms went largely ignored. As he reveals in "The Poet," this was his greatest artistic disappointment:

> He sang of love when earth was young,
> And Love, itself, was in his lays.
> But ah, the world, it turned to praise
> A jingle in a broken tongue.

Lavishly praised for his dialect poetry by well-meaning but misguided white critics, Dunbar was the first caged black bird of international fame to die beating his wings against the bars of racism.

But let us turn to how Dunbar and subsequent Black American poets adapted the ballad, sermon (i.e., the chanted versions), spirituals, gospel, blues, and jazz conventions to their needs. Whatever their avowed reasons for tapping the vein of folk art, the ultimate product, as I hope to demonstrate, reveals a nostalgic interest in folk life, an evaluation of Black folk values, the elevation of heroes among the Black masses and the validation of the Black vernacular as poetic material.

In her seminal studies of American culture, Constance Rourke reveals the complex relationships of the first popular American folk characters: the Yankee, the backwoodsman, and the Negro. After referring to the popularity of black-face minstrelsy in the 1830's as minor evidence of how "the comic trio tended to merge into a single generic figure," she wisely concludes that "each of the trio remained distinct."[6] Similarly, a close examination of the legends

49

of Brother Jonathan, Davy Crockett, Daniel Boone, and Paul Bunyan uncovers a different frame of reference than those of the ubiquitous Black preacher; John, the trickster slave; Harriet Tubman, the Moses of her people; and John Henry, the steel-driving man. It also reveals that the values affirmed in the Uncle Remus tales of Harris are not identical to those affirmed in the Uncle Julius tales of Chesnutt, and that Thomas Sutpen's vision of making it in America is opposed to that of the nameless narrator in *Invisible Man*. Whether in myth or character, the difference between white American folklore and Black American folklore is a difference of response to the racist nature of American life.

It is important to remember, however, that as products of a society in the state of ferment and flux, both Anglo-American and Afro-American folklore are marked by ambiguities. Insofar as both champion the values expressed in the American Creed, they are similar. But insofar as one is the lore of the oppressor, the white majority, and the other the lore of the victims of oppression, the Black Southerner and his Northern brothers, they are antithetical. On the one hand the basic values emanate from the preëminence of property, individualism and technology, while on the other they spring from the preëminence of the human spirit, social justice, and physical freedom.

I have shown that major Black writers and critics generally point to music as the mode through which folk art should inform Afro-American literature. But music and literature employ different modalities. And musicality in verse—when closely analyzed—turns out to be something entirely different from melody in music. First of all, the use of music might be either ornamental (superficial and external) or organic (structural and integral). That is, a poem like Eugene Perkins's "Ballad for a Folksinger" might have only a nominal and thematic affinity to the ballad tradition, while ballad conventions are inextricably woven into the structure and texture of a poem like Gwendolyn Brooks's "the ballad of chocolate Mabbie." Secondly, the conventions of folk music might be employed in the traditional manner of Dunbar's "An Ante-Bellum Sermon" or innovatively as in Miss Brooks's "The Sermon on the Warpland." And lastly, musicality in contemporary Afro-American poetry could mean either a careful arrangement of phonetic patterns and simple rhythmical effects as in Langston Hughes's "Boogie: 1 a.m." or soulful, surreal vibrations like those conveyed in Bob Kaufman's "Walking Parker Home."

In spite of its rather selective exclusion from early collections of Afro-American folksongs, the ballad has long been an influence on Black American poets. Since the late nineteenth century, Black folk have been singing of the exploits of Uncle Bud, Old Dog Blue, John Henry and The Rock Island Line. Traditionally, the folk ballad, usually rhyming *a b c b* in alternating tetrameter and trimeter lines, has been thought of as poetry of the people, by the people and for the people. Dunbar's "Black Samson of Brandywine" is among the early significant literary ballads. With full-throated pride, our Black bard of yesteryear sings the praises of the ebony giant of Delaware:

> There in the heat of the battle,
>   There in the stir of the fight,
> Loomed he, an ebony giant,
>   Black as the pinions of night.
> Swinging his scythe like a mower
>   Over a field of grain,
> Needless the care of the gleaners
>   Where he had passed amain.

The briefly described action and stock descriptive images of these stanzas are characteristic of the Scotch-English ballad, but, in the usual folk manner, Dunbar has freely adapted them to suit his ethnic and artistic purposes.

The ballad influence has been passed on from generation to generation by such landmarks as Countee Cullen's "Ballad of the Brown Girl" (hailed by Professor Kittredge as the finest literary ballad he had ever read), Langston Hughes's "Ballad of the Man Who's Gone" and "Ballad of the Landlord" (the poem that got a white Boston teacher fired), Sterling Brown's satirical saga of "Slim Greer" and "Ballad of Joe Meek" (which has a cutting edge and heroism all its own), Robert Hayden's messianic "The Ballad of Nat Turner," Melvin B. Tolson's zestful "The Birth of John Henry" and Dudley Randall's poignant "Ballad of Birmingham." All of the above employ traditional ballad formulas. Yet, except for Cullen's "Ballad of the Brown Girl," they pulsate with the historic tensions and spiritual vitality of the modern Black experience.

By and large the same is true of Miss Brooks's "A Bronzeville Mother Loiters in Mississippi. Meanwhile, a Mississippi Mother Burns Bacon" in *The World of Gwendolyn Brooks* and Sonia Sanchez's "a ballad for stirling street" in *We a BaddDDD People*. But these two poems also provide superb opportunities to examine the inventiveness of contemporary Afro-American ballads. Inspired by the lynching of 14-year-old Emmett Till for allegedly whistling at a white Mississippi housewife, "A Bronzeville Mother . . ." is an elaborate, free verse rendering of the wife's dramatic disenchantment with her husband's brutality. The ballad trappings are essentially ornamental. The Mississippi mother simply thinks of the bloody episode as like a ballad. She sees "Herself: the milk-white maid, the 'maidmild'/Of the ballad. Pursued/By the Dark Villain. Rescued by the Fine Prince." Aside from these stock ballad phrases, the abrupt opening and internal references to the ballad tradition, the poem is uniquely modern in spirit and style.

Miss Brooks brilliantly uses the turbulence of a domestic breakfast scene to reflect the tarnishing of her Southern maiden's dream. After burning the bacon, a symbolic referent to the tumultuous passions beneath the ostensible domestic tranquility, she has second thoughts about the Dark Villain:

> The fun was disturbed, then all but nullified
> When the Dark Villain was a blackish child
> Of fourteen, with eyes still too young to be dirty,
> And a mouth too young to have lost every reminder
> Of its infant softness.

And as she tries to refurbish her self-image as the beautiful wife worth "The gradual dulling of those Negro eyes," her image of the Fine Prince is completely destroyed when he viciously slaps their youngest child. As she looked "At her baby-child/She could think only of blood./Surely her baby's cheek/Had disappeared, and in its place, surely,/Hung a heaviness, a lengthening red, a red that had no end." Overcome by a wave of sickness, her mind flashes back to the courtroom scene and the "Decapitated exclamation points in that Other Woman's eyes." And in the closing stanzas, a hatred for the Fine Prince "burst into glorious flower." By the sheer force of her poetic imagination, Miss Brooks has assumed the persona of Southern White Womanhood and humanized it—which is no small feat for a Black mother/poet. And though the romantic resolution of the poem—the triumph of the individual conscience over the conscience of the community—may be at variance with the historical facts of lynching rituals, it is true to the tenor of the poem.

Miss Sanchez's "a ballad for stirling street" is another successful blend of old wine in new bottles. The inspiration for this ballad was a novel depicting the pathology of the Black life style on Newark, New Jersey's Howard Street. Miss Sanchez contrasts its images with the nationalistic vitality of Imamu Baraka's Stirling Street. Employing the "Lord Randall" ballad framework, the poet supplants the Scotch-English dialect and taut line with the Black vernacular and jazz rhythm:

> jest finished readen a book bout
>> howard street
> i've read a whole lot of books like
>> howard street
> if each one of us moved to a
>> howard street
> and worked hard like they do on
>> stirling street
> wudn't be no mo howard sts at all
> all the howard sts wud fall—fall—fall
> and won't that be good.
>>> yeh. yeh.
>>> and won't that be good.
>>> yeh. yeh. yeh.

This use of the refrain and incremental repetition represents the product of the historical cross between the ballad tradition of Europe and the unrhymed African call-and-response design.

The call-and-response was a favorite device of the slave exhorters and folk preachers. It was an outgrowth of a spirited exchange between the preacher and his congregation and a stock feature of chanted sermons: the highly rhythmic, imaginative and improvisational rendering of the Word of God. Dunbar's "An Ante-Bellum Sermon," James Weldon Johnson's poems in *God's Trombones* (1927), Hughes's "Sunday Morning Prophecy," Wright's parody of the "Train Sermon" in *Lawd Today* (1963), Ellison's incomparable fusion of "Let My People Go" and the "Train Sermon" in *Invisible Man* (1952), and Miss Brooks's "The Sermon on the Warpland" and "The Second Sermon on the Warpland," both in *In the Mecca* (1968), are among the major testimonials to the influence of the folk sermon.

Let us look at how the "Let My People Go" sermon was adapted by our Black bards. Dunbar's version in *Complete Poems* begins:

> We is gathahed hyeah, my brothas,
>   In dis howlin' wildaness,
> Fu' to speak some words of comfo't
>   To each othah in distress.
> An' we chooses fu' ouah subjic'
>   Dis—we'll 'splain it by an' by;
>   "An' de Lawd said, 'Moses, Moses,'
> An' de man said, 'Hyeah am I.'"

The folk idiom, the free-wheeling manner, the dramatic biblical imagery, and the syncopated rhythm are immediately captured in this opening stanza. Dunbar goes on to portray the shrewdness of the old exhorter as he manages to breathe fire into the spirits of his congregation while protecting himself from the treachery of Black Judases:

> So you see de Lawd's intention,
>   Evah sence de worl' began,
> Was dat His almighty freedom

Should belong to evah man,
But I think it would be bettah,
Ef I'd pause agin to say,
Dat I'm talkin' 'bout ouah freedom
In a Bibleistic way.

Unfortunately, this fine poem is conspicuously absent from nearly all anthologies by both Black and white editors.

When Johnson dropped the use of dialect in his version of "Let My People Go," he also deadened much of the spirit of the poem. His opening stanza reads:

And God called Moses from the burning bush,
He called in a still, small voice,
And he said: Moses—Moses—
And Moses listened,
And he answered and said:
Lord, here am I.

The biblical imagery and rhythm remain, but gone are the looser cadence and imaginative freshness of Dunbar's Black folk preacher. As Johnson continues the narrative of Moses's conflict with Pharaoh, he comes a bit closer to Black speech patterns:

Poor Old Pharaoh,
He knows all the knowledge of Egypt,
Yet he never knew—
He never knew
The one and the living God.
Poor Old Pharaoh,
He's got all the power of Egypt,
And he's going to try
To test his strength
With the might of the great Jehovah,
With the might of the Lord God of Hosts,
The Lord mighty in battle.
And God, sitting high up in his heaven,
Laughed at poor Old Pharaoh.

The recurring descriptive phrase "Poor Old Pharaoh," the repetition of words and beat in lines 3 and 4 and 10 and 11 as a kind of modified call-and-response device, and the picked-up tempo of this passage are traditional features of the chanted sermon.

Perhaps the best literary adaptation of antiphonal exchange in a sermon appears in the Prologue to *Invisible Man*. As the reader probably recalls, on the lowest level of the nameless protagonist's surreal descent into Dante's hell he hears the following:

> "Brothers and sisters, my text this morning is the 'Blackness of Blackness.'"
>
> And a congregation of voices answered: "That blackness is most black, brother, most black . . ."
> "In the beginning . . ."
> "At the very start," they cried.
> ". . . there was blackness . . ."
> "Preach it . . ."
> ". . . and the sun . . ."
> "The sun, Lawd . . ."
> ". . . was bloody red . . ."
> "Red . . ."
> "Now black is . . ." the preacher shouted.
> "Bloody . . ."
> "I said black is . . ."
> "Preach it, brother . . ."
> ". . . an' black ain't . . ."
> "Red, Lawd, red: He said it's red!"
> "Amen, brother . . ."

For those readers who are not attuned to the frequencies of folk sermons and therefore fail to sense the distinctive spell-binding qualities of this passage, it would be instructive to compare it with Faulkner's handling of a Black sermon in *The Sound and the Fury*.

The Reverend Homer Barbee's sermon is another masterpiece of poetic creativity. I will not go into the whole panoply of rich details that Ellison weaves into this episode, which runs some fourteen pages, from the Reverend's round, vibrant voice and rhythmic rocking motion to his more vigorous pacing back and forth on the platform as he reaches the climactic moments of his delivery. Let me simply point out that after intoning his comparison of the Black Founder of the college with "the humble carpenter of Nazareth" and "that great pilot of ancient times who led his people safe and unharmed across the bottom of the blood-red sea," Reverend Barbee rolls into the metaphorical rendering of the Founder's death:

> "In the car up ahead, in the Pullman assigned him by the very president of the line, the Leader lay tossing. He had been struck with a sudden and mysterious sickness. And I knew in spite of the anguish within me that the sun goeth down, for the heavens themselves conveyed that knowledge. The rush of the train, the clicking of wheels upon the steel. I remember how I looked out of the frosted pane and saw the looming great North Star and lost it, as though the sky had shut its eye. The train was curving the mountain, the engine loping like a great black hound, parallel with the last careening cars, panting forth its pale white vapor as it hurled us ever higher. And shortly the sky was black without a moon. . . . It was as though the very constellations knew our impending sorrow. . . . For against that great-wide-sweep of sable there came the burst of a single jewel-like star, and I saw it shimmer, and break, and streak down the cheek of that coal-black sky like a reluctant and solitary tear. . . ." He shook his head with great emotion, his lips pursed as he moaned, "Mmmmm-mmmmmm. . . . At that fateful moment . . . Mmmmmm, I sat with your great president . . . Mmmmmmmmmm!"

Other parallels to the "Train Sermon" are legion, but none is more powerful than Ellison's literary version.

Like the chanted sermons, the spirituals are characterized by improvised graphic phrases and dramatic lines that are usually delivered in a call-and-response formula. But in form and content the range is wide, with poets as different as Dunbar and Curtis Mayfield finding ample variety to suit their tastes. Dunbar's "A Spiritual" has the common structure of four-line stanzas with four beats in each line and a refrain:

> Oh, sinnah, mou'nin' in de dusty road,
> Hyeah's de minute fu' to dry yo' eye:
> Dey's a mouthy One a-comin' fu' to baih yo' load;
> Lif' up yo' haid w'en de King go by!

Stock folk references to Jesus as "Capting," "Mastah," "a moughty One" and "King," along with the recurring emotional expletive "Oh" and the use of rhyme, contribute to the distinctive, soulful quality of these lines. A more plaintive poem by Dunbar which also bears the indelible imprint of the spirituals is "W'en I Gits Home," whose closing stanza pleads for God's call:

> Oh, Mastah, won't you sen' de call?
> My frien's is daih, my hope, my all.
> I's waitin' whaih de road is rough,
> I want to hyeah you say,
>   "Enough,
>   Ol' man, come home!"

Even in these melancholic lines one discerns this facet of Dunbar's mood and technique that is unmatched by his white contemporaries.

A more recent example of how the spirituals were used by a Black American poet is Waring Cuney's "My Lord, What a Morning," included in Rosey Pool's *Beyond the Blues* (1962). The title and chorus of Cuney's poem is a direct borrowing from the spiritual "My Lord, What a Mornin'." The traditional

> My Lord, what a mornin',
> My Lord, what a mornin',
> My Lord, what a mornin',
> When de stars begin to fall
>   (chorus repeated)

becomes the modern

> Oh, my Lord
> What a morning,
> Oh, my Lord,
> What a feeling,
> When Jack Johnson
> Turned Jim Jeffries'
> Snow-white face
> Up to the ceiling.
> Yes, my Lord,
> Fighting is wrong,
> But what an uppercut.
> Oh, my Lord,
> What a morning.

Beneath the literary surface of this poem, the vitality of folk art still lives.

Curtis Mayfield's "We're Rolling On" in A. X. Nicholas's *The Poetry of Soul* (1971) is apparently a secularized version of the spiritual "I'm A-Rolling," collected in James Weldon Johnson and J. Rosamond Johnson's *The Book of American Negro Spirituals* (1925). At any rate, there is a parallel between the titles, refrains and imagery of the two lyrics which suggests the thin line between the Songs of the Lord and what the old folks called the Devil Tunes. Thus the refrain "Cause we're rolling on, we're rolling on, we're rolling on, we're rolling on" harks back to "I'm a rollin', I'm a rollin', I'm a rollin' through an unfriendly worl'." Both bear witness to life as a hard road to travel. The difference between the sacred and the secular versions is that the latter are more assertive, more inventive and looser in rhythm.

Actually, the rhythmic and improvisational characteristics of Mayfield's lyrics are more in tune with the freer style and driving beat of gospel music, the sacred counterpart of the urban blues. If we look closely at Mayfield's "Keep on Pushin' " and "We're a Winner" we will discover borrowings from Mahalia Jackson's "Move on up a Little Higher." However, the changes he makes are dramatic. For example, contrast Miss Jackson's joyous but otherworldly "One of these mornings,/One of these mornings/I'm gonna lay down my cross/And get my crown" with the resoluteness of Mayfield's slangy "Keep on pushin',/Keep on pushin',/I've got to keep on pushin'/I can't stop now." And contrast the mood of

> Move on up a little higher,
> Meet my friends and kindred.
> Move on up a little higher,
> Meet that Lily of the Valley,
> Feast with the Rose of Sharon.

with the lines:

> We're a winner
> And never let anybody say

59

Boy, you can't make it
'Cause a feeble mind is in your way
No more tears do we cry
And we have finally dried our eyes
And we're movin' on up
Movin' on up
Lord have mercy, we're movin' on up
Movin, on up.

The key figures of speech might be similar, but the rap is quite different.

Nikki Giovanni's rap on the gospel album "Truth Is on Its Way" is also quite different. With the soul-stirring singing of the New York Community Choir in the background, Miss Giovanni reaches the young and the old with her message. The most moving of the poems on this album for me is "The Great Pax Whitie," with its refrain "peace be still" blending harmoniously with the hymn with which it is paired, "Peace Be Still." The match-up of "My Tower" with "Pretty Little Baby" is also successful. But several of the other pairings of poems and vocal music are less felicitous. The themes, moods, rhythms, idioms and images in marriages like "This Little Light of Mine" with "Second Rapp Poem" are, at best, amusingly incompatible. The image of the fiery Rapp Brown as a little light just does not come across for me. But whether Miss Giovanni is rappin' or poetin' her album has opened new vistas for her celebrated talents. And as did Langston Hughes, who began the technique of reading poems to the background of choir music, she is moving on up.

The strong, rocking beat, ambiguous imagery, and wide tonal range of the gospels are largely derived from Thomas A. Dorsey (alias Georgia Tom on the chitterling circuit) and the influence of the blues. For that matter, all contemporary Black American music is rooted in the blues or the spirituals. Structurally, the blues generally takes the form of three-lines stanzas rhyming *a a b* with four beats in each line. But since the blues has few absolute features, there are many variations on this form. Stylistically, the blues lyricist employs stock imagistic phrases like "The eagle flies on

Friday, and Saturday I go out to play," stock interjections like "Oh, Baby" and "Yes, Lord" (used in call-and-response manner with accompanying instrumental improvisation), repetition and occasional moans, growls and shouts. In theme and mood the blues is a lyrical expression of hard times and the possibility of overcoming personal misery through toughness of spirit.

A highly prolific and versatile artist, Langston Hughes drew heavily on Afro-American folk music for inspiration and technique. His first book of verse focuses on the night life of the Harlem cabarets and captures the sights and sounds of the Jazz Age. "Midnight Nan at Leroy's," "Young Singer," "Nude Young Dancers," and "Black Dancer in the Little Savoy" are poems revealing the most important characters in *The Weary Blues* (1926). Reflecting the hollowness of white America and the synthetic joy of Harlemites, "The rhythm of life/Is a jazz rhythm" to which the "night dark girl of the swaying hips" dances while the "sleek black boys" watch. The only sound to break the jazz rhythm is the occasional "aching emptiness" of the blues like that being sung by the Black piano player in the title poem:

> In a deep song voice with a melancholy tone
> I heard that Negro sing, that old piano moan—
>   "Ain't got nobody in all this world,
>   Ain't got nobody but ma self.
>   I's gwine to quit ma frownin'
>   And put ma troubles on the shelf."
> Thump, thump, thump, went his foot on the floor.
> He played a few chords ther   sang some more—
>   "I got the Weary Blues
>   And I can't be satisfied.
>   Got the Weary Blues
>   And can't be satisfied—
>   And I wish that I had died."
> And far into the night he croor   'nat tune.
> The stars went out and so did tl   oon.

Original in form and superb in execution, "The Weary Blues" is outstanding literary art in the folk motif.

More recent examples of Hughes's poems in the blues

motif are found in his *Selected Poems* (1959). Some are humorously domestic like "Morning After" and "Early Evening Quarrel"; others are funereal, like "Widow Woman" and "Young Gal's Blues"; and still others, like "Bound No'th Blues" and "Same in Blues," treat various aspects of a dream deferred. "The Backlash Blues" in *The Panther and the Lash* (1967) provides an instructive contemporary illustration of Hughes's versatile use of the blues form. The poem deals with the "white backlash," a media term describing the hostile reactions of white folk to civil rights activities. Personifying his topic as Mister Backlash (a satirical title that reverberates down the corridors of the Black experience from the traditional cynicism about Mister Charlie to Jean Knight's rhythm-and-blues tune "Mr. Big Stuff"), Hughes addresses him:

> You give me second-class houses,
> Give me second-class schools,
> Second-class houses
> And second-class schools.
> You must think us colored folks
> Are second-class fools.

Here the poet breaks down the conventional three-line stanza, of which the second line is a restatement of the first and the third line is a contrasting statement, into a six-line stanza. But Hughes maintains the terseness and cutting edge of the blues style. The sting comes in the closing lines:

> Mister Backlash, Mister Backlash,
> What do you think I got to lose?
> Tell me, Mister Backlash,
> What you think I got to lose?
> I'm gonna leave you, Mister Backlash,
> Singing your mean old backlash blues.
> > *You're the one*
> > *Yes, you're the one*
> > *Will have the blues.*

The coda, of course, is a special Hughes touch which subtly though ambiguously underscores the apocalyptic tone of the last stanza. Thus, the music of Hughes's poetry conveys the sound of Lenox Avenue, Seventh Street and South State Street. And his language has been appropriately called Harlemese: vibrant, rhythmic, direct and racy.

The contemporary poets who have been influenced by Hughes and the blues tradition are legion: Tom Weatherly, A. B. Spellman, Sonia Sanchez, Ted Joans, Stanley Crouch, Bob Kaufman, Al Young, Tom Dent, Michael Harper, Carolyn Rodgers, Don Lee, Sam Greenlee, Eugene Perkins and Eugene Redmond—to name a few. In many instances, the influence is ornamental and thematic, as in Miss Sanchez's "for our lady," Kaufman's "Blues Note," Young's "A Dance for Ma Rainey," Dent's "Ray Charles at Mississippi State," Miss Rodgers's "Song to U. of C.—Midway Blues," Greenlee's "Blues for an African Princess" and Perkins's "Blues." Sometimes the blues mood is more ritualistic and intrinsic, as in Baraka's "Rio's New Blues," Lee's "Sun House" and Harper's "Village Blues." And at other times the new poets experiment with the blues motif and form, as Crouch does in his short "Blues, for Sallie," Joans in the tongue-in-cheek "Little Brown Bitch Blues (or; I've Got the Sun in My Soul)," and Redmond in the seven-part soliloquy "Spearo's Blues (Or: Ode to a Grecian Yearn)."

Perhaps the best example of an innovative take-off on the blues model by a contemporary Black American poet is Ted Joans's "Passed on Blues: Homage to a Poet." In sixteen free-style four-line stanzas rhyming *a b c c,* Joans pays tribute to the poet laureate of Black America. Except for the refrain "That was the world of Langston Hughes," the metrical patterns and line lengths vary from stanza to stanza. And occasionally Joans throws in a five-line stanza:

the elephant laugh
the rain forest giggles under a switchblade downpour
the zoot suited conked head razor throat Stompin' at the Savoy
the colored newspaper with no good news
That was the world of Langston Hughes

After cataloguing the sights, sounds, smells and very soul of Hughes's Harlem, Joans wraps up his homage with:

63

the sweaty hard-working muscle making black back breaking
    hard labour hump
the bold bright colors on ebony nappy head big titty itty
    bitty Liza Jane
the millions and millions raising up strong been done
    wrong too long pointing
the abused body at slum lord! war lord! police lord!
    Oh Lord, all guilty and accused!
THAT WAS THE WORLD OF THE POET LANGSTON
    HUGHES
    BLACK DUES! BLACK BLUES! BLACK NEWS!
THAT WAS THE WORLD OF THE GREATEST BLACK
    POET
    LANGSTON HUGHES

Like the blues singer in his choice of language and form,
Joans's major consideration is that his song should feel and
sound "right" to him. That "Passed on Blues: Homage to
a Poet" obviously does (note the fascinating alliteration and
assonance at the end of the above lines) is a tribute to Joans
as well as part of Joans's tribute to Langston Hughes and
the blues.

More conventional yet still organic uses of the blues
tradition occur in Tom Weatherly's "blues for franks woot-
en" and A. B. Spellman's "The Joel Blues." The risqué
closing stanza of Weatherly's four-stanza poem employs
typical blues imagery with a highly personal touch:

let me be your woodpecker mama tom do like no pecker would.
let me be your woodpecker mama tom tom do like no pecker
    would.
open your front door baby black dark come home for good.

Spellman also makes use of sensual imagery and phrases
common to the tradition:

            i'm a easy riding papa
            i'm your everloving so & so.
            i'm a easy riding papa
            i'm your everloving so & so.
                don't think i don't hear you calling
                cause i'm coming when you want to go.

64

Clearly, this generation of poets has drunk from the wells of Afro-American folk music.

It is not surprising, therefore, that in addition to adopting folk ballads, sermons, spirituals, gospels and the blues, many of the new Black poets have incorporated jazz motifs into their poems. The intense four-beats-to-the-measure rhythm coupled with syncopation—the trademark of early jazz—is an outgrowth of the blues tradition. In fact, as Eileen Southern points out in *The Music of Black Americans: A History* (1971), the most salient features of jazz derive directly from the blues. The jazz artist attempts to recreate the singing style of the blues singer and—in the case of the avant-garde, like Archie Shepp—the voice of the urban ghetto with scooping, sliding, whining, growling and falsetto effects on his instrument. Like the blues, jazz uses the call-and-response style with the antiphonal relationship occurring between two solo instruments or between solo and ensemble. And in jazz as in the blues a traditional melody or harmonic framework serves as the takeoff point for improvisation—either solo or collective. More recently, as the new sound of John Coltrane, Ornette Coleman, Cecil Taylor and Miles Davis indicates, the trend has been toward collective improvisation and a freer polyphonic textured music. For poets this new Black music opens new vistas on the use of language.

As revealed above, Langston Hughes was the first to introduce the rhythms of jazz into poetry. And his range includes not only the syncopated beat of his poems collected in the Twenties but also the boogie beat of his poems from the Forties and Fifties. Listen, for example, to the sound of "Boogie: 1 a.m.":

> Good evening, daddy!
> I know you've heard
> The boogie-woogie rumble
> Of a dream deferred
> Trilling the treble
> And twining the bass
> Into midnight ruffles
> Of cat-gut lace.

and the first stanza of "Lady's Boogie":

> See that lady
> Dressed so fine?
> She ain't got boogie-woogie
> On her mind—

And when we turn to contemporary poet/politician Julian Bond's "Look at That Gal . . .":

> Look at that gal shake that thing.
> We cannot all be Martin Luther King,

we are again confronted by the legacy of Langston Hughes and Afro-American jazz.

Each of the contemporary Black American poets who drew on jazz for inspiration and/or technique added his or her own personal touch. Such is the case with Miss Brooks's swinging treatment of "The Sundays of Satin-Legs Smith," in which Satin-Legs "wakes, unwinds, elaborately: a cat/ Tawny, reluctant, royal. He is fat"; and in "We Real Cool," the tragically hip brothers "Jazz June" but "Die soon." Waring Cuney works out a bopping style in "Charles Parker, 1925-1955." Dig how he blows: "Listen,/That there/Is what/Charlie/Did/To the Blues./This here,/bid-dle-dee-dee/bid-dle-dee-dee/have you any cool?/bahdada/one horn full./Charlie/Filled the Blues/With/Curly-cues./ That's what/Charlie/Did/To the Blues." Cuney obviously knows how to scat with the best of them. (Note the humorous improvisation and onomatopeia of the above lines.) Moving on to Don Lee's "But He Was Cool or: he even stopped for green lights," we hear yet another sound:

> cool-cool is so cool he was un-cooled by
>   other niggers' cool
> cool-cool ultracool was bop-cool/ice box
>   cool so cool cold cool
> his wine didn't have to be cooled, him was
>   air conditioned cool
> cool-cool/real cool made me cool—now
>   ain't that cool
> cool-cool so cool him nick-named refrigerator.

Here Lee revels in the rich cadences and nuances of Black street language. Jiving, bopping, rapping, signifying, sounding—all modes of Afro-American expression—seek to affirm the vitality of the Black American experience, to expand the limits of language and to display the speaker's soul power.

What is soul? Well, it is hard to define but not difficult to recognize. As the brother on the block would say, to have soul is knowing how to walk that walk and talk that talk; how to get down to the nitty gritty and work with the grits and greens; how to tell it like it is and keep on pushing; how to be what you are and believe in what you do. To have soul is getting your thing together and sharing it with your brothers and sisters—those who have paid their dues, Black or white, and are delivering the news. In other words, soul power is the primal force of human nature, tempered by a common experience of suffering and struggle for survival that manifests itself through shared modes of perceiving and expressing that experience; it is, above all, the affirmation of the resiliency of the spirit—the inner experience—in a world of insecurity and blues-like absurdity.

If we again apply our convenient but by no means mutually exclusive classifications of ornamental and organic to the use of jazz by this generation of Black poets, we discover that only a few poems fall into the first category. Salient among these are the humorous, rhythmic put-ons and put-downs in Ted Joans's "Uh Huh" and "Stormy Monday Girls" and Don Lee's "Reflections on a Lost Love" and "blackmusic/a beginning." The large majority of contemporary jazz poems bridge the gap between the merely thematic and rhythmic and the more vital stylistic and improvisational forms of jazz. Some are impassioned treatments of the music or its devotees, like Conrad Kent Rivers's "Underground," Joans's "Jazz Is My Religion," Eugene Perkins's "Jazz Poem" and Bob Kaufman's "Bagel Jazz," "Tequila Jazz," "Jazz Chick," "O—Jazz—O" and "O—Jazz—O War Memoir. . . ." Others are thematically more concerned with the giants in jazz, as illustrated in David Henderson's "A Coltrane Memorial," Sonia Sanchez's "A/Coltrane Poem," Carolyn Rodgers's "Written for Love of an Ascension—Coltrane," Joans's "Jazz Must Be a Woman" and "In Homage to Heavy Loaded Trane, J. C.," Kaufman's "Mingus" and "Walking Parker Home," and Michael Harper's "Yusef Iman," "For Bud," "Mr. P. C.," "Brother John," "Dirge for Trane" and "Dear John, Dear Coltrane."

As the above suggests, the most inspirational musician is the late John Coltrane and the most prolific and outstanding contemporary stylists in jazz poetry are Kaufman, Joans and Harper. Kaufman was a leading light of the West Coast beat generation, but his first book, *Solitudes Crowded with Loneliness,* was not published until 1965. Joans is a nomad in the arts, a world traveler and one of Langston Hughes's many protégés. His *Black Pow-Wow,* dedicated "To Langston Hughes and allyall," was published in 1969. Of East Coast origins but West Coast orientation, Harper is a long-time jazz devotee and a young academician. His first book, *Dear John, Dear Coltrane,* came off the press in 1970.

The style, energy and illumination of the poems in each of these books attest to the varied backgrounds and prodigious talents of the poets. Take the first two stanzas of Kaufman's "Mingus":

> String-chewing bass player,
> Plucking rolled balls of sound
> From the jazz-scented night.
>
> Feeding hungry beat seekers
> Finger-shaped heartbeats,
> Driving ivory nails
> Into their greedy eyes.

If it is true that the late André Breton, a founder of the surrealist movement, considered Ted Joans the only Afro-American surrealist, he apparently had not read Kaufman. (At any rate, he had much to learn about Afro-American poetry.) The direct simplicity of the closing lines of "Jazz Is My Religion" is also a salient feature of Joans's poetry:

So remember that JAZZ is my religion
but it can be your religion too but JAZZ is a truth that is always
black and blue Hallelujah I love JAZZ so Hallelujah I dig JAZZ
so
Yeah JAZZ IS MY RELIGION

The middle section of Harper's "Dear John, Dear Coltrane" bears witness to the finely honed, Black-based quality of his poetry:

> Dawn comes and you cook
> up the thick sin 'tween
> impotence and death, fuel
> the tenor sax cannibal
> heart, genitals and sweat
> that makes you clean—
> *a love supreme, a love supreme*
> *Why you so black?*
> *cause I am*
> *Why you so funky?*
> *cause I am*
> *Why you so black?*
> *cause I am*
> *Why you so sweet?*
> *cause I am*
> *Why you so black?*
> *cause I am*
> *a love supreme, a love supreme*

The sound and sense of these lines express the quintessence of soul power.

I have attempted to demonstrate how folk art is introduced into contemporary Afro-American poetry. By literary history, analysis, analogy and example, I have shown that regardless of the socio-political convictions of individual members of this generation of Black poets, a considerable number of their poems reveal a romantic interest in and realistic evaluation of Black folk values, a celebration of the Black masses and of musicians as heroes, and a validation of the poetic qualities of Black speech and Black music. My argument does not stand or fall on a rigid definition of folk art as unwritten material. For while it is true that all of the contemporary poems examined are "literary," they nevertheless pulsate with the vibrancy and fluidity of folk art. More importantly, the internal evidence reveals that they are poems created by Black people, about Black people and, in the main, for Black people first, and then for the world.

Notes

INTRODUCTION

1. *The Book of American Negro Poetry,* rev. ed. (New York: Harcourt, Brace & World, 1959), p. 9.
2. See, for example, Richard Wright, "Blueprint for Negro Literature," *Amistad 2,* eds. John A. Williams and Charles F. Harris (New York: Vintage Books, 1971), p. 5; LeRoi Jones, "The Myth of a Negro Literature," *Home: Social Essays* (New York: Apollo Edition, 1966), pp. 105-115; David Littlejohn, *Black on White: A Critical Survey of Writing by American Negroes* (New York: Viking Compass Book, 1969), pp. 3-65; C. W. E. Bigsby (Baltimore: Pelican Book, 1971), pp. 5-33; and Nathan Irvin Huggins, *Harlem Renaissance* (New York: Oxford University Press, 1971), p. 5. For an interesting commentary on Jones's indictment of Black literature, see Cecil M. Brown, "Black Literature and LeRoi Jones," *Black World,* XIX, (June 1970), 24-31.
3. Third edition (New York: Harvest Book, 1956), p. 22.
4. Quoted in Vernon Hall, Jr., *A Short History of Literary Criticism* (New York: New York University Press, 1963), pp. 7-8.
5. *Ibid.,* pp. 12-14.
6. Wellek and Warren, *Theory of Literature,* p. 31.

CHAPTER I

1. *The Roots of American Culture and Other Essays,* ed. Van Wyck Brooks (New York: Harvest Book, 1942), pp. 22-26.
2. Bluestein, *The Voice of the Folk* (Massachusetts: University of Massachusetts Press, 1972), pp. 16-64.
3. *Ibid.,* p. 7.
4. Quoted in Bluestein, p. 6.
5. (Oxford: Clarendon Press, 1965), p. 70.
6. *Ibid,* p. 142.
7. *Ibid.,* p. 70.
8. *Ibid.,* p. 74.
9. *Ibid.,* p. 105.
10. *Ibid.,* p. 124.
11. Quoted in Bluestein, p. 8.
12. Bluestein, p. 16.
13. Quoted in Bluestein, p. 38.

CHAPTER II

1. See *The English and Scottish Popular Ballads,* 5 vols. (Boston and New York: Houghton Mifflin, 1882-1898). Reprinted 1956.

2. See *Old English Ballads* (Boston: Ginn, 1894), *The Beginnings of Poetry* (New York: Macmillan, 1901), and *Democracy and Poetry* (Boston and New York: Houghton Mifflin, 1911).
3. See the Introduction, *The English and Scottish Popular Ballads,* abridged ed. (Boston: Houghton Mifflin, 1904), pp. xi-xxi. Reprinted 1932.
4. (New Brunswick, New Jersey: Rutgers University Press, 1959), p. 4.
5. Wilgus, p. 7.
6. *Idem.*
7. *Ibid.,* p. 32.
8. P. xxi.
9. Quoted in Wilgus, p. 34.
10. See Melville J. Herskovits, *The Myth of the Negro Past* (Boston: Beacon Press, 1958).
11. W. E. B. DuBois, *Dusk of Dawn* (New York: Schocken, 1968), p. 47.
12. F. M. Barnard, *Herder's Social and Political Thought* (Oxford: Clarendon Press, 1965), pp. xiii-xiv.
13. Quoted by Saunders Redding, Introduction, *The Souls of Black Folk* (New York: Crest Book, 1961), p. ix.
14. *The Souls of Black Folk,* p. 181.
15. *Ibid.,* p. 188.
16. See, for example, *The New Negro* (New York: Atheneum Edition, 1968), *Four Negro Poets* (New York: Simon and Schuster, 1927), *The Negro and His Music* (Washington: Associates in Negro Folk Education, 1936), and *The Negro in Art* (Washington: Associates in Negro Folk Education, 1940).
17. *The New Negro,* p. 47.
18. *Idem.*
19. *Ibid.,* p. 48.
20. *Ibid.,* pp. 48-49.
21. *Ibid.,* p. 51.
22. "The Negro Spirituals," *The New Negro,* p. 199.
23. *Ibid.,* p. 200.
24. *Ibid.,* p. 201.
25. *Ibid.,* p. 204.
26. *The New Negro,* p. 7.
27. Johnson took considerable pride in his matrilineal West Indian ancestry, and one of his tutors was a West Indian cobbler whose command of the English language and classical literature was impeccable. See James Weldon Johnson, *Along This Way: The Autobiography of James Weldon Johnson* (New York: The Viking Press, 1933), pp. 6-7, 92-93.
28. *Along This Way,* pp. 10-25.
29. *Ibid.,* p. 13.

30. *Ibid.,* p. 158.
31. (New York: Viking Compass Edition, 1969), p. 5. Two perceptive studies of the folk preacher are Henry H. Mitchell, *Black Preaching* (New York: J. B. Lippincott, 1970), and Bruce A. Rosenberg, *The Art of the American Folk Preacher* (New York: Oxford University Press, 1970).
32. James Weldon Johnson and J. Rosamond Johnson, eds., *The Book of American Negro Spirituals* (New York: Viking Compass Edition, 1969), p. 23.
33. For an intriguing attempt to relate the spirituals and sermons to Albert B. Lord's formulaic theory of oral composition, see Rosenberg (note 31).
34. Johnson argued that ragtime was originated by colored piano players in the "questionable resorts" along the Mississippi River. "Once the text of all Ragtime songs was written in Negro dialect," he states, "and was about Negroes in the cabin or in the cotton fields or on the levee or at a jubilee or on Sixth Avenue or at a ball, and about their love affairs. Today, only a small proportion of Ragtime songs relate at all to the Negro. . . . But that does not abolish in any way the claim of the American Negro as its originator" *(The Book of American Negro Poetry,* p. 12).
35. P. 20. My italics.
36. *Ibid.,* p. 41-42.
37. Quoted by Mercer Cook and Stephen Henderson, *The Militant Black Writer in Africa and the United States,* (Madison: University of Wisconsin Press, 1969), p. 5.
38. Robert W. July, *A History of the African People* (New York: Charles Scribner's Sons, 1970), p. 356.
39. See Robert W. July, *The Origins of Modern African Thought* (New York: Praeger, 1967).

CHAPTER III

1. Other major Black writers who fared well include Langston Hughes, Gwendolyn Brooks, Countee Cullen, and James Baldwin. See "Black Writers' Views on Literary Lions and Values," *Negro Digest,* XVII (January 1968), 10-48, 81-89.
2. *Amistad 2,* p. 5.
3. *Ibid.,* p. 6.
4. *Idem.*
5. *Ibid.,* p. 7.
6. (Garden City, New York: Doubleday Anchor Book, 1964), p. 84.
7. *Idem.*
8. *Amistad 2,* p. 10.
9. *Ibid.,* pp. 12-13.

10. A voracious reader and self-educated man, Wright was guided in his reading by Dr. Louis Wirth, a well-known sociologist at the University of Chicago. Also, in his Introduction to Horace Cayton and St. Clair Drake's *Black Metropolis,* Wright states that "it was from the scientific findings of men like the late Robert E. Park, Robert Redfield, and Louis Wirth that I drew the meanings for my documentary book *12 Million Black Voices;* for my novel, *Native Son;* it was from their scientific facts that I absorbed some of the quota of inspiration necessary for me to write *Uncle Tom's Children* and *Black Boy,*" revised edition, Vol. I (New York: Harbinger Book, 1962), p. xviii. See also "Reflections on Richard Wright: A Symposium on an Exiled Native Son," *Anger and Beyond,* ed. Herbert Hill (New York: Perennial Library Edition, 1968), pp. 196-212.

11. See Langston Hughes, "The Twenties: Harlem and Its Negritude," *African Forum,* I (Spring, 1966), 11 and Johnson, *Along This Way,* pp. 158-160.

12. "Living with Music," *Shadow and Act* (New York: Random House, 1964), p. 190. Italics in original.

13. Ellison, "Hidden Name and Complex Fate," *Shadow and Act,* pp. 159-160.

14. *Ibid.,* p. 171.

15. *Ibid.,* p. 172.

16. For the most significant controversial study establishing white sources for the Afro-American spirituals, see George Pullen Jackson, *White and Negro Spirituals* (New York: J. J. Augustin, 1943). The definitive history of the spirituals, including a refutation of the Jackson study, is John Lovell, Jr., *Black Song: The Forge and the Flame* (New York : The Macmillan Company, 1972).

17. *Shadow and Act.,* p. 255.

18. *Ibid.,* p. 172.

19. *Ibid.,* p. 173.

20. *Ibid.,* p. 217.

21. *Ibid.,* p. 246.

22. *Ibid.,* pp. 245-246.

23. *Ibid.,* p. 244.

24. *Ibid.,* p. 239.

25. *Ibid.,* p. 234.

26. *Ibid.,* pp. 58-59.

27. *Ibid.,* pp. 103-104.

28. LeRoi Jones, *Black Music* (New York: Apollo Edition, 1968), p. 16.

29. Professor Theodore Hudson of D. C. Teachers College has recently completed a biographical and critical work on Imamu Amiri Baraka that is as intriguing as it is timely. It is soon to

be published by Duke University Press. According to Professor Hudson, Baraka did not graduate from Columbia with an M.A.

30. LeRoi Jones, "How You Sound," *The New American Poetry,* ed. Donald M. Allen (New York: Evergreen Books, 1960), p. 425.
31. *Ibid.,* p. 424.
32. Jones, *Home,* p. 10.
33. Jones, *Black Music,* p. 185.
34. Jones, *Home,* p. 245. See also Edward Sapir, "Culture, Genuine and Spurious," *Selected Writings of Edward Sapir in Language, Culture and Personality,* ed. David G. Mandelbaum (Berkeley and Los Angeles: University of California Press, 1968), pp. 308-331.
35. *Home,* pp. 111-112.
36. *Ibid.,* p. 112.
37. *Ibid.,* p. 113.
38. *Ibid.,* p. 246.
39. Barnard, p. 142.
40. Nathan Glazer and Daniel Moynihan, *Beyond the Melting Pot* (Cambridge, Massachusetts: The M.I.T. Press, 1964), p. 51.
41. (New York: Oxford University Press, 1964), p. 29. It should be noted that Gordon's theory of ethnic group structure is one of the principal underpinnings in two important studies of Afro-American culture. See Harold Cruse, *The Crisis of the Negro Intellectual* (New York: Apollo Edition, 1968), pp. 8-10 and Andrew Billingsley, *Black Families in White America* (New Jersey: Prentice-Hall, 1967), pp. 6-10.

CHAPTER IV

1. *The Roots of American Culture and Other Essays,* p. 26.
2. Actually the pioneer scholarship was done by Professor Child. Kittredge was his student and, later, his friend and colleague. See Notes 1 and 3, Chapter II.
3. See "A Conversation with Leopold Senghor," *Negro Digest,* XVI (May 1967). Also see Lilyan Kesteloot, *Les écrivains noirs de langue francaise: naissance d'une littérature,* 4th edition (Brussels: Free University of Brussels, 1971), pp. 63-81.
4. *Home,* p. 110.
5. *Ibid.,* p. 115.
6. *American Humor: A Study of the National Character* (New York: Doubleday Anchor Book, 1931), pp. 88-89.

Bibliography

Barnard, F. M. *Herder's Social and Political Thought*. Oxford: Clarendon Press, 1965.

Bell, Bernard W., ed. *Modern and Contemporary Afro-American Poetry*. Boston: Allyn and Bacon, 1972.

Bigsby, C. W. E., ed. *The Black American Writer*. Vol. I. Pelican Book. Baltimore: Penguin Books, 1971.

Billingsley, Andrew. *Black Families in White America*. New Jersey: Prentice-Hall, 1967.

"Black Writers' Views on Literary Lions and Values." *Negro Digest,* XVII (January, 1968), 10-48 and 81-89.

Bluestein, Gene. *The Voices of the Folk: Folklore and American Literary Theory*. Massachusetts: University of Massachusetts Press, 1972.

Brooks, Gwendolyn. *The World of Gwendolyn Brooks*. New York: Harper and Row, 1971.

Brown, Cecil M. "Black Literature and LeRoi Jones." *Black World,* XIX (June, 1970), 24-31.

Brown, Sterling A. *Southern Road*. New York: Harcourt, Brace, 1932.

——————, Arthur P. Davis and Ulysses Lee, eds. *The Negro Caravan: Writings by American Negroes*. New York: Arno-New York Times Reprint, 1970.

Chapman, Abraham. *Black Voices*. Mentor Book. New York: New American Library, 1968.

Charters, Samuel. *The Poetry of the Blues*. New York: Avon Books, 1970.

Child, Francis James. *The English and Scottish Popular Ballads*. 5 vols. Boston and New York: Houghton Mifflin, 1882-1898. Reprinted 1956.

"A Conversation with Leopold Senghor," *Negro Digest*, XVI (May 1967), 26-35.

Cook, Mercer and Stephen Henderson. *The Militant Black Writer in Africa and the United States*. Madison: University of Wisconsin Press, 1969.

Coombs, Orde, ed. *We Speak As Liberators: Young Black Poets*. New York: Dodd, Mead, 1970.

Cruse, Harold. *The Crisis of the Negro Intellectual*. New York: Apollo Editions, 1968.

DuBois, William E. B. *Dusk of Dawn*. New York: Schocken Edition, 1968.

——————. *The Souls of Black Folk*. Crest Book. New York: Fawcett World Library, 1961.

Dunbar, Paul Laurence. *The Complete Poems of Paul Laurence Dunbar*. New York: Apollo Editions, 1969.

Ellison, Ralph W. *Invisible Man*. Signet Book. New York: New American Library, 1952.

——————. *Shadow and Act*. New York: Random House, 1964.

Giovanni, Nikki, *Black Feeling, Black Talk, Black Judgment*, New York: William Morrow, 1970.

——————. *Re:Creation*. Detroit: Broadside Press, 1970.

——————. *Truth Is on Its Way*. New York: Right on Records, 1971.

Glazer, Nathan and Daniel Moynihan. *Beyond the Melting Pot*. Cambridge: M. I. T. Press, 1964.

Greenlee, Sam. *Blues for an African Princess*. Chicago: Third World Press, 1971.

Gummere, Francis Barton. *Democracy and Poetry*. Boston and New York: Houghton Mifflin, 1911.

——————. *The Beginnings of Poetry*. New York: Macmillan, 1901.

——————. *Old English Ballads*. Boston: Ginn, 1894.

Hall, Vernon, Jr. *A Short History of Literary Criticism*. New York: New York University Press, 1963.

Harper, Michael S. *Dear John, Dear Coltrane.* Pittsburgh: University of Pittsburgh Press, 1970.

Hayden, Robert. *Selected Poems.* New York: October House, 1966.

——————. *Words in the Mourning Time.* New York: October House, 1970.

Herskovits, Melville J. *The Myth of the Negro Past.* Boston: Beacon Press, 1958.

Hill, Herbert, ed. *Anger and Beyond: The Negro Writer in the United States.* Perennial Library Edition. New York: Harper & Row, 1968.

Huggins, Nathan Irvin. *Harlem Renaissance.* New York: Oxford University Press, 1971.

Hughes, Langston. *The Panther and the Lash: Poems of Our Times.* New York: Alfred A. Knopf, 1967.

——————, "The Twenties: Harlem and Its Negritude." *African Forum, 1* (Spring, 1966), 11-20.

——————. *Selected Poems of Langston Hughes.* New York: Alfred A. Knopf, 1959.

——————. *The Weary Blues.* New York: Alfred A. Knopf, 1926.

—————— and Arna Bontemps, eds. *The Poetry of the Negro, 1746-1970.* New York: Doubleday, 1970.

Jackson, George Pullen. *White and Negro Spirituals.* New York: J. J. Augustin, 1939.

Jeffers, Lance. *My Blackness Is the Beauty of This Land.* Detroit: Broadside Press, 1971.

Joans, Ted. *Black Pow-Wow.* New York: Hill and Wang, 1969.

Johnson, James Weldon, *Along This Way: The Autobiography of James Weldon Johnson.* New York: Viking Press, 1933.

——————, ed. *The Book of American Negro Poetry.* Rev. ed. New York: Harcourt, Brace and World, 1959.

——————. *God's Trombones: Seven Negro Sermons in Verse.* Compass Book. New York: Viking Press, 1969.

Jones, LeRoi (Imamu Amiri Baraka). *Black Magic: Collected Poetry, 1961-1967.* New York: Bobbs-Merrill, 1969.

——————. *Black Music.* New York: Apollo Editions, 1968.

——————. *Home: Social Essays.* New York: Apollo Editions, 1966.

——————. "How You Sound." *The New American Poetry,* ed. Donald M. Allen. Evergreen Book. New York: Grove Press, 1960.

—————— and Larry Neal eds. *Black Fire: An Anthology of Afro-American Writing.* New York: Apollo Editions, 1969.

July, Robert W. *A History of the African People.* New York: Charles Scribner's Sons, 1970.

——————. *The Origins of Modern African Thought.* New York: Praeger, 1967.

Kaufman, Bob. *Solitudes Crowded with Loneliness.* New York: New Directions, 1965.

Kesteloot, Lilyan. *Les écrivains noirs de langue française: naissance d'une littérature.* 4th ed. Brussels: Free University of Brussels, 1971.

Kittredge, George Lyman and Helen Child Sargent. *The English and Scottish Popular Ballads.* Abridged ed. Boston: Houghton Mifflin, 1904. Reprinted 1932.

Lee, Don L. *Don't Cry, Scream.* Detroit: Broadside Press, 1969.

——————. *We Walk the Way of the New World.* Detroit: Broadside Press, 1970.

Littlejohn, David. *Black on White: A Critical Survey of Writing by American Negroes.* Compass Book. New York: Viking Press, 1969.

Locke, Alain Leroy. *Four Negro Poets.* New York: Simon and ,Schuster, 1927.

——————. *The Negro and His Music.* Washington: Associates in Negro Folk Education, 1936.

——————. *The Negro in Art.* Washington: Associates in Negro Folk Education, 1940.

——————. *The New Negro.* New York: Atheneum Publishers, 1968.

Lovell, John, Jr. *Black Song: The Forge and the Flame, The Story of How the Afro-American Spiritual Was Hammered Out.* New York: Macmillan, 1972.

Mitchell, Henry H. *Black Preaching.* New York: J. B. Lippincott, 1970.

Nicholas, A. X., ed. *The Poetry of Soul.* New York: Bantam Books, 1971.

Perkins, Eugene. *Black Is Beautiful.* Chicago: Free Black Press, 1968.

Pool, Rosey E. *Beyond the Blues: New Poems by American Negroes.* Kent, England: Hand and Flower Press, 1962.

Randall, Dudley, ed. *The Black Poets.* New York: Bantam Books, 1971.

Rosenberg, Bruce A. *The Art of the American Folk Preacher.* New York: Oxford University Press, 1970.

Rourke, Constance. *American Humor: A Study of the National Character.* Anchor Book. New York: Doubleday, 1931.

——————. *Roots of American Culture, and Other Essays.* Ed. (posthumous) Van Wyck Brooks. Harvest Book. New York: Harcourt, Brace & World, 1942.

Sanchez, Sonia. *Homecoming*. Detroit: Broadside Press, 1968.

—————. *We a BaddDDD People*. Detroit: Broadside Press, 1970.

Sapir, Edward. "Culture, Genuine and Spurious." *Selected Writings of Edward Sapir in Language, Culture and Personality*. Ed. David G. Mandelbaum. Berkeley: University of California Press, 1968, pp. 308-331.

Southern, Eileen. *The Music of Black Americans: A History*. New York: W. W. Norton, 1971.

Wellek, René and Austin Warren. *Theory of Literature,* 3rd ed. Harvest Book. New York: Harcourt, Brace & World, 1956.

Wilentz, Ted and Tom Weatherly. *Natural Process*. New York: Hill and Wang, 1970.

Wilgus, D. K. *Anglo-American Folksong Scholarship Since 1898*. New Brunswick: Rutgers University Press, 1969.

Williams, John A. and Charles F. Harris, eds. *Amistad 2: Writings on Black History and Culture*. Vintage Book. New York: Random House, 1971.

Wright, Richard. "Introduction." St. Clair Drake and Horace R. Cayton. *Black Metropolis: A Study of Negro Life in a Northern City*. Vol. I. New York: Harcourt, Brace and World ,1945.

—————. *Lawd Today*. New York: Avon Books, 1963.